Hoop Tales:

Tennessee Lady Volunteers

Randy Moore

INSIDERS' GUIDE®

GUILFORD, CONNECTICUT
AN IMPRINT OF THE GLOBE PEQUOT PRESS

INSIDERS' GUIDE®

Text design: Casey Shain
Cover photos: *front cover:* Tamika Catchings (Greg Ditmore); *back
cover:* top, 1973–74 team (*Knoxville News-Sentinel*); bottom, Pat
Summitt (Randy Moore/*Rocky Top News*).

Library of Congress Cataloging-in-Publication Data
Moore, Randy, 1952-
    Hoop tales : Tennessee Lady Volunteers / Randy Moore. — 1st ed.
        p. cm. — (Hoop tales series)
ISBN 0-7627-3703-4
    1. University of Tennessee, Knoxville—Basketball. 2. Lady Volun-
    teers (Basketball team) I. Title: Tennessee Lady Volunteers. II. Title.
    III. Series.

GV885.43.U58M67 2005
796.323'63'0976885—dc22   2005046139

Manufactured in the United States of America
First Edition/First Printing

Contents

Dedication

For my mother— a gentle spirit, a dear friend, and a true blessing.

Acknowledgments

Special thanks to Debbie Jennings, Rob Turner, and the rest of the Lady Vol sports information staff for their tremendous help on this project.

Introduction

I began my journalism career at the *Knoxville Journal* the same month that Pat Head began her coaching career at the University of Tennessee. Lady Vol basketball was one of my first assignments, giving me a rare opportunity to follow Head's program on its remarkable rise from obscurity to national prominence.

The pages that follow offer a first-hand look at the coaches, athletes, and administrators who helped mold Tennessee into the model program in women's basketball.

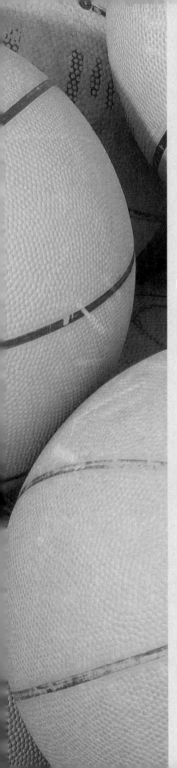

The Early Years

Barely two dozen females were enrolled at the University of Tennessee in 1903, but their impact would prove much larger than their number. Noting the presence of a women's basketball program at nearby Maryville College, they complained vehemently regarding the absence of such a program on The Hill. Exasperated, school officials made a small concession to silence them: The young ladies could use the campus gymnasium from 4:00 to 6:00 P.M. one day per week.

According to the 1903 school yearbook, the team consisted of seven "varsity" members: captain Katherine Williams, manager Laura Thornburgh, Fannie DeGolia, Blanch McIntire, Mary Treadwell, Maude Keller, and Jane Williams. The yearbook also listed five "scrubs": Jessie McKay, Mabel Fair, Jessie Swann, Jennie Buquo, and Harriet Baumann.

School records indicate the loosely organized team competed twice that season. The squad played a modified form of basketball

The group that started it all—the 1903 Tennessee women's basketball team.
University of Tennessee Special Collections

in which three forwards played exclusively on the offensive end of the court, while three guards played exclusively on the defensive end. This supposedly would protect fragile young ladies from the injuries sure to occur if they were forced to run from one end of the court to the other. Regardless, Tennessee's women debuted with a 10–1 loss at Maryville College on March 13 and fell 16–6 in an April 6 rematch at Knoxville.

When the 1904 team also lost both of its games, Tennessee's players realized they were missing something—a team cheer, perhaps. They had one in place by the time the 1905 season rolled around:

"Hippity-hus! Hippity-hus!

"What in the thunder's the matter with us?

"Nothing at all! Nothing at all!

"We are the girls who play basketball."

When the 1905 team lost all four of its games, it became apparent the program needed more than a cheer; it needed a catchy motto. The players eventually came up with one: "'Twas not so much dishonor to be beaten as 'tis an honor to have struggled."

Sadly, the '06 squad dishonored itself by going 0–3, dropping Tennessee's all-time mark in women's basketball competition to an uninspiring 0–11.

Thanks to some clever scheduling, the program finally made a breakthrough in 1907. Tennessee opened that season with a 28–0 pasting of nearby Central High School. Unfortunately, the momentum—and the season—ended eleven days later with a 22–11 loss at Maryville.

In 1908 coach Clyde Burnley was entrusted with keeping an eye on the program, literally (he had lost an eye in a chemistry-class explosion). The captain of the team was Grace Livingston

The 1906 team, resplendent in middy blouses and bloomers. University of Tennessee Special Collections

Hood, a versatile young lady who also was elected to be secretary-treasurer and poet for the senior class. In addition, she was vice president of the boat club, a group of six daring young women who had the unmitigated gall to go rowing—unescorted, no less—down the Tennessee River. The '08 hoops squad prevailed in just one of its three outings (beating Central High again) despite the sterling play of Hood, who was recognized as "Best Basketball Player—Girl."

The 1909 season brought two milestones. The team registered the program's first tie, playing the Tennessee Deaf and Dumb

School (now the Tennessee School for the Deaf) to a 12–12 stalemate in the opener. It also recorded the first non-losing season in program history, going 1–1–1. The win, of course, came at the expense of Central High.

Just as the program appeared to be building some momentum, adversity struck. A 0–2 record in 1910 left Tennessee's all-time record in women's basketball competition at a none-too-sterling 3–17–1. Worse, the losses came at the hands of perennial whipping boy Central High (21–1) and Knoxville High (6–4). The program promptly was disbanded, and it would remain dormant for nine years.

Women's varsity hoops returned to the University of Tennessee in 1920, this time known as the Pioneer Girls Basketball Team. After losing its first three games, the squad rallied vigorously—blasting Knoxville YWCA 30–1 and Martha Washington 18–10 to finish 2–3. A full schedule reportedly was arranged for 1921 but was abruptly canceled "due to disorganization."

Coach Mabel Miller revived the program in 1922. School records suggest the team played two games in the state of Kentucky, winning 28–19 at Cumberland College before losing 14–8 at Union College. But Hattie Carothers (Stanfill) insists the team played three games, and she should know. She was a starting guard that season.

"I remember we went by train and played at three different small colleges," she said in a 1999 interview at age ninety-eight. "The people were very friendly to us, and we stayed in small hotels. Riding on a train was a big thing for me and the [other] players, too."

Unmarried at the time, Carothers played exclusively on defense in those days of a divided court for women. "I didn't have a

GIRL'S BASKET BALL

Josephine Reddick

Yell

Hippity-hus! Hippity-hus!
What in the Thunder's the matter with us?
Nothing at all! Nothing at all!
We are the girls who play basket ball!

Motto-:-"Twas not so much dishonor to be beaten as 'tis an honor to have struggled."

'Varsity

MARGARET PERKINS (Manager)	Center
MABEL GILDERSLEEVE	Right Forward
GRACE HOOD	Left Forward
DAISY WADE	Right Guard
ESSIE POLK (Captain)	Left Guard

Substitutes

BERTHA ROSE MILLER	ANNA WEYLAND
NANNIE TODE	MARY COOPER

The 1906 Volunteer yearbook recognized girls' basketball but misspelled it.
University of Tennessee Special Collections

chance to shoot goals," she recalled, "which was a good thing, because I had such bad eyesight."

What she lacked in vision, she more than offset with aggressiveness and savvy. Carothers, by her own account, was a defensive dynamo. "I found out I could do little things to make that person that I was guarding mad," she recalled. "And when they were mad, they didn't shoot goals well. . . . I liked to guard the tall ones because I was short. I would get up under her arms and do a little dance that wouldn't be called a foul. They would get mad and miss."

During her days at Centerville High School, the energetic Miss Carothers once guarded an opponent so zealously, the exasperated foe lashed out at her verbally. "She got mad and said, 'I'm not a mule!'" Stanfill recalled eight decades later. "That pleased me."

The attire of the time was not exactly designed for comfort or ventilation. "We wore great big black bloomers and socks that were rolled down," Stanfill said. "Also, middy blouses with a sailor collar that stretched down and reached over our hips. Our athletic shoes were hand-laced."

Then, as now, those who played varsity sports were accorded respect and attention—the women as well as the men. Downtown merchants often gave athletes discount rates on various items, Stanfill noted.

Earning a varsity letter was a big deal in those days. Upon receiving hers at "a big meeting in a big building," Stanfill recalled "running down the aisle, hollering" in celebration. Amused teammates "laughed and clapped" at her energetic antics. Conversely, university males found her varsity letter downright confounding. "When I wore my letter on my sweater, the boys wanted to know where I bought it," she said. "I didn't look like I could play, since I was only 5-foot-4 and always wore glasses. They just couldn't believe I could earn a letter playing basketball."

Hattie helped the 1923 team post the first winning record in program history, sweeping its first three games before dropping a 15–12 heartbreaker to Sullins College in the season finale. A writer for the school yearbook, *The Volunteer*, was lavish in praise of the team, noting: "The proof of the strength of the girls' basketball team is evident in the results of the games. The colleges played were Cumberland, Carson-Newman, Martha Washington and Sullins. Out of this number, only one game was lost. The success of this year's team will do much to establish basketball as a major sport among the coeds."

Not really. Consider this item from the 1924 edition of *The Volunteer*: "When the time came for activity around the baskets in Jefferson Hall, the outlook for the girls was dreary. The edict had gone forth, 'There will be no Inter-Collegiate competition in Girls' Basketball.' However, this proclamation was recalled as unauthorized, and thanks to the action taken by the Athletic Council, Basketball stands as an established sport at the University."

Once the '24 team was cleared to compete, Fay Morgan assumed the coaching reins and posted a 4–3 record that included a high-scoring (for that era) 48–24 rout of Cumberland College. *The Volunteer* called the season "clearly the most eventful one in the history of the cage game for girls on the Hill."

That 1924 team, nicknamed the Volettes, featured forty-five varsity candidates at the first practice. By the time the season began, all but sixteen young ladies had departed or been released.

Apparently operating on the premise "If you can't beat 'em, hire 'em," Tennessee lured Ann Huddle to coach its 1925 team. Huddle had coached East Tennessee Normal School (later East Tennessee State University) to the championship of East Tennessee/Southwest Virginia in 1924, and one of her signature victories had been a 22–16 season-opening defeat of the Volettes. Given this interesting twist, emotions surely ran high when Huddle took her new team (Tennessee) to face her old team (Normal) on February 2, 1925, in Johnson City. The hotly contested game ended, appropriately enough, in a 25–25 tie.

After a 5–3–1 record in her first season at Knoxville, Huddle got the Volettes clicking in 1926. *The Volunteer* recapped the season with these words: "Despite the many predictions that the University of Tennessee would not have a successful Co-ed basketball season, Coach Ann Huddle brought her comparatively green team through an eight-game schedule with seven victories."

Huddle's team breezed through its first seven games—winning by an average of 29 points per contest—before dropping the season finale to Maryville by a 28–27 score. *The Volunteer* gushed praise for the team: "The forwards were all fast and shifty, and accurate in shooting goals and in passing. On the defense, the guards covered their opponents very cleverly, and seldom let them have possession of the ball for more than a moment. A wealth of reserve material was a great asset to the team."

Incredibly, just as the program finally was gaining widespread popularity, school officials ordered it disbanded again. As before, the culprit was the perception that women were too frail to play a game as physically taxing as basketball. Strangely enough, though, school officials replaced women's varsity basketball with a host of intramural sports—basketball, tennis, volleyball, hockey, soccer, riflery, horseback-riding, hiking, stunts, folk and interpretive dancing, swimming, golf, and track.

After two years spent overseeing the various intramural programs, Huddle left the university to attend Columbia Teachers College. In 1978, precisely fifty years later, she wistfully recalled the dissolution of the women's basketball program with these words: "The local high schools had tournaments at UT, and there were some injuries, after which the men's department at UT felt that women should no longer play basketball. An athletic committee, under Dean [Nathan] Dougherty's leadership, decided it was for the best interest of the women to discontinue the basketball program."

Silly? Certainly. Nevertheless, thirty-two years would pass before women's basketball would return as a varsity sport on The Hill.

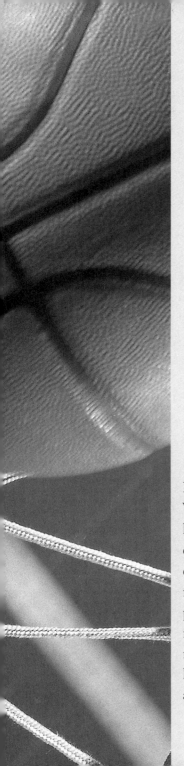

Shooting Down Chauvinism

Nancy Lay was not a happy camper. Her Volettes had played a good first half against homestanding Carson-Newman College, only to be told they could not finish the game on the main gym floor. The Carson-Newman men's team was using the gym for its pregame warm-ups and had no intention of relinquishing the court. Banished to the basement of the building, the two women's teams had no choice but to conclude their game on a lesser court. Demeaning as it was, the incident would not be Lay's most lasting memory of that evening.

"There was a track above the gym where we played the second half," she recalled. "One time the ball was passed to Brenda Green, and I yelled for her to shoot. When she did, the ball hit the underside of the track, then came down and hit Brenda in the head, knocking her out cold."

Four decades later, Lay still laughs at the recollection. The teams she coached from 1960 to 1968 endured a lot of growing pains, but they also enjoyed a lot of laughs while laying the groundwork for what was to become the dominant program in women's collegiate basketball: the Tennessee Lady Vols.

When the University of Tennessee restored women's basketball as a varsity sport in 1960, Lay was a logical choice to coach the team. First of all, she had led the movement to revive the program following a thirty-four-year hiatus. Secondly, she had played at the high school level and also at the University of Richmond, one of precious few colleges to field a women's team. Third, she had been overseeing Tennessee's intramural basketball program for several years. Last, but not least, she was a real bargain. "I got around $3,000 as a full-time teacher," she recalled. "I never got anything for coaching."

Although it took place amid the civil rights movement, the Vietnam War, feminism, Watergate, and the other social upheavals that marked the 1960s, the return of women's hoops on The Hill would prove very significant in its own right. The rebirth can be attributed to the Tennessee College Women's Sports Federation (TCWSF), the women's liberation movement, and a few odd twists of fate.

"It was happenstance," recalled Lay, a university professor whose love for basketball was surpassed only by her love for teaching. "Women's basketball basically emanated from our club sports program, featuring physical education majors who were looking for some kind of intercollegiate experience. They wanted to play other schools, and other schools felt the same way."

First, though, Lay and other members of the TCWSF had to convince college administrators across the state to upgrade women's basketball from club sport to varsity sport. Their quest met surprisingly little opposition. "The TCWSF was the impetus for intercollegiate basketball in the state," she said. "We had to put some pressure on but there was not a lot of opposition. It was still basically a club sport, and that's the way it was funded."

Naturally, there was too much bureaucracy in place for change to occur smoothly. The movement to restore women's basketball had to cut through miles of red tape.

"There were lots of hearings regarding the program and what it should be like," Lay said. "A commission studied it for quite a long time. Finally, the commission decided women's athletics should be run like men's athletics . . . with one featured program." At Tennessee, the featured men's program was football. The featured women's program, the committee decided, should be basketball. And, as Lay noted, "The rest is history."

As with any new endeavor, women's basketball met with plenty of obstacles. The first one—finding some players—proved much more difficult than expected. "The toughest thing was generating some interest among the students," Lay said. "Some of the better players preferred intramurals because they were in sororities and didn't want to spend the extra time it would take to practice for the varsity. Physical education majors were the backbone of the program, although they weren't necessarily the most skilled players."

Nancy Lay revived women's basketball at Tennessee and served as
coach from 1960 to 1968.
University of Tennessee Photography Center

While finding players was difficult, finding controversy was not. "This was a time of women's liberation," Lay noted, "so some feminist factions on campus wanted different school colors for the women's team. They didn't want the women to wear the same colors as the men." This idea was never taken seriously, however, and the women eventually adopted orange and white as their team colors—not that it really mattered. "We didn't have uniforms," Lay recalled. "The players just wore shorts and T-shirts."

In addition to no uniforms, the Volettes had no means of transportation and no funding. "The players paid their own way everywhere we went," Lay said, "and they paid entry fees to get in tournaments."

Because there was no money available for travel expenses, Tennessee played a close-to-home schedule in those days. The opponents included mostly in-state schools such as Maryville College (20 miles away), Carson-Newman (30 miles), East Tennessee State University (80 miles), and Chattanooga (100 miles). Still, Lay never viewed scheduling as an obstacle.

"Competition is competition," she said. "Everybody wants to win. Those teams played with as much spirit and heart as anyone today . . . just not as much skill."

Not as much publicity, either. In a very real sense, this was the prehistoric era of women's basketball. There were no sports information offices to generate interest in the teams or even to record results of the games. To this day the Lady Vols' annual media guide lists Lay as the coach from 1960 through 1968 but offers no further information on those seasons—not one player, not one score, not one opponent. It's as if the program didn't exist. It did, of course, but even the head coach's memory of those bygone days is a bit fuzzy.

"I don't remember the first practice, the first game, or the first win," Lay said. "I really don't remember much about those days. It was all about the game. People just loved the sport, so publicity was no big deal."

Although she has limited memories of that era, Lay has fond memories of the players she coached. Two of her favorites were Brenda Green, who was knocked out by the ricocheting basketball at Carson-Newman, and Barbara Brimi, who went on to become dean of the business school at Knoxville's South College. "They were two really great people and really great players," Lay stated.

The coach also recalls Jane Smart (Knoxville), Jackie Watson (Cookeville), and Nancy Bowman as quality players in those early years.

Since no records were kept of Tennessee's scores during the 1960s, there is no way to know how many points the Volettes produced or how many games they won. Still, Lay suspects her teams were more potent offensively than many teams of that era. "We scored a lot," she said. "There were no puny scores. We'd usually score 50 points or more."

Even in those primitive, formative years, the Volettes managed to foster one intensely heated rivalry. Tennessee Tech, located ninety minutes away in Cookeville, had developed a superior program under the direction of Marynell Meadors. Whenever the Volettes and Golden Eaglettes collided, the crowds were bigger, the coaches more animated, the games more fiercely competitive, and the memories more vivid than usual.

"The highlight of my first year was when Tennessee Tech came to Knoxville," Lay said. "Marynell Meadors was a great coach, and it was a huge rivalry. The gym was packed."

You Think You've Got It Tough?

When Barbara Brimi boarded an Austin, Texas, elevator one day in the mid-1980s, she found herself surrounded by tall and trim young women. She quickly discovered they were members of the Lady Vols basketball program, in town to play the University of Texas Lady Longhorns.

Brimi felt an immediate kinship with these young women. After all, she had played at Tennessee in the 1960s, when the program was in its infancy. Of course, times were harder then. Players supplied their own shoes, drove their own cars to road games, paid for their own meals, and even chipped in on tournament entry fees. They often played two games in a single day and almost always drove back to campus immediately after playing. Still, she and her teammates were so grateful for the opportunity to compete they never complained about the inconveniences.

By the time she exited the elevator, however, Brimi's elation had turned to frustration. She would share these feelings with her former coach, Nancy Lay, in a telephone conversation hours later.

"Barbara told me she was on an elevator with several Lady Vols," Lay recalled, "and they were actually complaining about having to take a Delta Airlines flight. That just shows how times have changed."

A pioneer of the Tennessee women's basketball program, Brimi helped blaze the trail for those who followed. Having driven her own car to road games back in the 1960s, she couldn't muster a whole lot of sympathy for modern-day counterparts whining about the school's choice of airlines.

"Those early players don't get much recognition for paving the way," Lay noted. "They tend to resent the fact the kids today aren't appreciative of all the opportunities they have."

Still, Lay's strongest recollection concerns a sidelight that had no bearing whatsoever on the game itself. "They brought their mascot [a guy dressed in a Golden Eagle outfit], and it rode around the gym floor on a scooter," Lay said, laughing at the recollection forty-five years later. "I don't remember the score or even who won, but I remember that mascot on that scooter."

Another of the bizarre memories she clings to concerns the low-budget gifts her players received for special achievements. "We gave awards for winning a tournament or something like that," Lay recalled. "One time we gave toenail clippers! They were like a hundred for a dollar. A few years later, I actually had someone mail a pair of those old clippers back to me!"

Due to haphazard record-keeping and faded memories, Lay's eight seasons overseeing Tennessee's program can never be adequately recorded for posterity. Accurately recapping her most significant victories and her most heartbreaking defeats simply is not possible. Suffice to say, she found the experience exciting, challenging, and rewarding. Still, she realized following the 1968 season that it was time to step aside. A new day in women's basketball was dawning, and she simply did not wish to be a part of it.

"I like to teach, and I didn't want to get into big-time athletics," she said. "I knew what was coming; it was going to become a full-time job, and I didn't want that. I didn't even apply for the job. I just wanted to get out. I didn't like anything about it when it got to be big-time."

When women's basketball was still a part-time job in a small-time atmosphere, however, no one found the experience more exhilarating than Nancy Lay. "I never regretted any of that," she said. "I had a wonderful career at UT; everybody was always

It Just Wasn't Ladylike

The old ways sometimes die slowly. Nancy Lay discovered as much following her eight-year tenure as head coach of the Tennessee women's basketball program.

In those chauvinistic times, school officials considered females too fragile to play full-court basketball. Instead, they played a game known as rover basketball. Each team featured two forwards who played on the offensive end of the floor, two guards who played on the defensive end, and two rovers who could roam about freely.

After stepping down as head coach in 1968, Lay spent two years securing her master's degree at Florida State University, then returned to Knoxville. She was surprised to find virtually nothing had changed in the hoops program during the interim.

"When I came back to Tennessee in 1970 to pursue my doctorate, they were still playing rover," she remembered. "When I asked why, they said women weren't physically or mentally strong enough to play full-court . . . and it wasn't ladylike, either. I told them I was thirty-seven years old, and I had played full-court at Florida State without any problem."

Her objections were duly noted and then quickly forgotten. Tennessee continued to play rover basketball for several years. Lay could only shake her head in befuddlement. "It was all about perception," she said. "There were some odd perceptions in those days regarding what women could and could not do."

supportive. But I always much preferred just to teach. For me, it was very stressful to coach.

"But I loved basketball. Still do."

Lay's love for the game is well documented. After stepping down as coach, she agreed to serve as UT's coordinator of women's sports for several years. In this capacity she was partially responsible for the hiring of Pat Head in 1974, a move that proved to be a watershed event in program history.

Lay, whose interest in academics always exceeded her interest in sports, was crossing campus one evening in the fall of 1974 when she noticed the lights were on at Alumni Gym. Stepping inside to investigate, she found Head making her coaching debut before a crowd that could be counted on the fingers of two hands. In fact, it could be counted on the thumbs.

"Mr. Pease [custodian Doug Pease] was there and I was there but I don't remember anybody else," Lay recalled, unable to stifle a chuckle. "And I just sort of wandered in. Pat was all dressed up; she was upset that I was dressed like a hippie. I was her boss, actually; that was the irony of the whole thing."

Although Head lost her debut as Tennessee's coach that evening, Lay was unconcerned. In her mind, there was a much more important game on the schedule.

"I hated Memphis State," she said. "We never did have very good luck with them when I was coach. They were much more organized than we were; we kind of practiced haphazardly. Anyway, Pat was getting ready for a game at Memphis in 1974, and I told her, 'If you don't beat Memphis State, don't come back.'"

During the eight years Lay served as Tennessee's coach, her heftiest operating budget was $500. Head's budget wasn't appre-

Making Dough from Doughnuts

Having spent most of the 1960s as head coach of the women's basketball team at Tennessee, Nancy Lay knew funding the program was always a challenge. That's why she could appreciate the initiative shown by one of her successors.

Coach Margaret Hutson convinced *The Daily Beacon*, Tennessee's student newspaper, to print a lengthy article publicizing the fact that the 1973–74 Volettes were selling doughnuts to raise funds for their upcoming season. Duly impressed by this bold marketing strategy, Lay sought out the coach to offer congratulations and to get a progress report. When she asked how much response the newspaper article had generated, however, Lay was not ready for Hutson's response.

"Not much," Margaret replied. "Somebody called and wanted to sell me a doughnut-maker."

ciably better in 1974 and 1975, but a change would be forthcoming in 1976. That was the year legislation known as Title IX assured women equal opportunities in athletics at federally funded schools. Tennessee's administration had been fairly supportive of women's sports in the 1960s and early 1970s, but now school brass was ready to put its money where its mouth was.

"Right after Title IX passed, they [school officials] were afraid they would be sued, so they came up with $10,000 to fund our seven women's sports," Lay recalled. "I was the women's sports coordinator, so I doled out the money. Everybody got the same amount [roughly $1,428]."

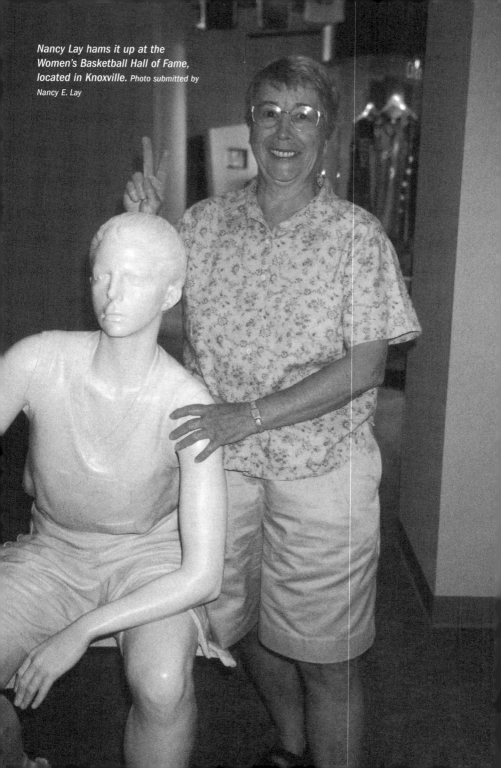

Instead of $1,428, the Lady Vols now have a seven-figure operating budget. Instead of a 3,000-seat gym, the team now plays in a 24,000-seat arena. Instead of crowds that can be counted on the fingers, the team routinely plays before turnouts of 10,000 to 15,000 and occasionally records a sellout. Instead of being a well-kept secret, the team now has every game broadcast on radio and a half-dozen per season aired on television—*national* television.

Naturally, Nancy Lay never dared to dream of such lofty accomplishments when she assumed the reins forty-five years ago. "I didn't see this. I really didn't," she said, her voice filled with pride. "I remember asking Pat one time: 'What do you envision?' She said, 'I want to fill the arena. That's my one big goal.' And she's done that. She's ideally suited for the job."

Of course, Nancy Lay was ideally suited for the job back in 1960. After a thirty-four-year hiatus, women's basketball on The Hill needed someone with determination, energy, and vision to guide the program through difficult times. By doing so, Nancy Lay laid the foundation for the incredible success that would follow.

" . . . and the Volettes Won"

It had been a long day. And it was going to be an even longer night. After driving to Rock Hill, North Carolina, on the morning of February 15, 1969, Tennessee's Volettes had beaten Georgia 38–26 that afternoon and then come back that evening to nip the host Winthrop team 31–29.

Having won the prestigious Winthrop Invitational, Tennessee's players were eager to shower, slip into their street clothes, and pile into their cars for the long drive back to Knoxville. When they opened the gym door, however, they were chilled to the bone by the frigid temperatures. Worse, they found roughly 18 inches of snow blanketing the countryside. It was, they learned later, the area's worst snowstorm in more than a century.

The only way back home was the winding two-lane roads that snaked their way through the Great Smoky Mountains—roads so icy and treacherous they would require days of melting before they were passable again. Tennessee's players would not be going home anytime soon.

"They're just going to have to miss classes," head coach Joan Cronan mused as she peered out at the snow-covered landscape. "We'll have to stay here for a while."

The decision to stay put was easy; there was no other viable option. But the coach faced another decision that would be much more difficult: Where would the Volettes sleep? With a mere $500 annual budget, Cronan could not afford to pay for lodging. After conferring with some Winthrop officials, the coach broke the news to her players. "The roads are impassable," she said, "and we don't have money for motel rooms. We'll be staying at a recreation lodge here on campus."

Several players groaned. Several smiled. Several just stared blankly at the coach, unsure how to react. One Volette asked to use the telephone and placed a collect call to her hometown. "Mom, we're snowed in, and I don't have any money," the player said, pausing briefly before cheerily adding: "But Mrs. Cronan doesn't, either, so we'll be okay."

Huddled around a fireplace, Cronan and her players spent the night curled up on the floor of the lodge, nestled in sleeping bags borrowed from female students. Three days would pass

Making a Difference

When twelve-year-old Joan Cowart showed up at Little League baseball tryouts in Opelousas, Louisiana, back in the late 1950s, one of the coaches told her politely but firmly: "You can't try out because you're a girl." Young Cowart frowned, then turned and strode angrily from the park. From that moment on, she dedicated her life to righting this wrong by creating greater athletic opportunities for females. "I will make a difference someday," she vowed.

Roughly a decade later, she coached volleyball, basketball, and tennis at Northwestern Louisiana, subsequently adding the title of women's athletics director. By 1968 she was coach of the University of Tennessee women's basketball team. By 1981 she was the school's women's athletics director. By 1990 her program was considered the model for women's athletics departments across America.

The twelve-year-old girl who had been told she couldn't try out for Little League had indeed "made a difference." Her married name? Joan Cowart Cronan.

before those icy mountain roads were safe enough to allow the Volettes to make the return trip to Knoxville.

That blizzard made such an impression on one Tennessee player, Jane Hill, it was still vividly etched in her memory thirty-six years later. "There was probably 15 to 20 inches of snow," she said. "It was the largest they'd had there in over a hundred years . . . just an incredible snowstorm. There was no way for us to get out. We couldn't get two steps out of the lodge."

Hill was one of the true pioneers of Tennessee women's basketball. Growing up in Dandridge, she led tiny Maury High School (since phased out) to the state championship as a senior in 1966, earning tournament Most Valuable Player recognition in the process. There were no college scholarships available for women in those pre–Title IX days, but Hill attracted some attention nonetheless. "I was recruited by Nashville Business College, which was basically a semipro team," she recalled. "The team played internationally—against the Russians and teams like that."

Hill also got an offer to attend Nashville's Peabody Teachers College (now part of Vanderbilt University). She even got an offer from the Arkansas Redheads, a touring team that essentially featured white women performing the same type of colorful antics black men were doing for the Harlem Globetrotters. "I still said no," she recalled. "I was going to UT."

At Tennessee, Hill played number-one singles for the tennis program, started for the volleyball program, and revolutionized the basketball program. The first Volette to elevate herself while shooting, she would be known as "Jump-Shot Jane" throughout her college career. "I was only 5-feet-6," she said. "That's why I developed the jump shot."

Joan Cronan became the
Lady Vols head coach in
1968 at the age of
twenty-three. *UT Women's
Media Relations*

Because the Tennessee Secondary School Athletics Association considered full-court basketball too taxing for girls, Hill had to play the antiquated six-on-six half-court game in high school. Each team featured three forwards, who played exclusively on the offensive end of the court, and three guards, who played exclusively on the defensive end.

Due to a perception that college women were almost as fragile as high school girls, the University of Tennessee offered a modified version of the half-court game, rover basketball, with two forwards, two guards, and two rovers who were free to roam all over the court.

Hill limited herself to tennis and volleyball until her junior year. When she finally showed up for basketball tryouts, she was surprised by the sparse turnout. "We didn't have more than ten or twelve show up," she recalled. "It was not that selective."

It was not that important, either. Women's basketball at the college level was essentially a club sport. "College ball was not as serious at that time as high school ball had been," Hill noted. "We were really trained in high school, and I was serious about basketball then. But at the college level it was more like intramurals. We had no scholarships and no travel budget; we drove our own cars to the games. We had uniforms, and that was it."

Hill remembers her college coach as being young and pretty, yet fiercely competitive in her approach to the game. "Joan Cronan was this attractive young woman only about three or four years older than some of her players," Hill said. "She was easy-going and fun to be with, but you knew when she said something she meant it. You respected her."

The players respected her so much, in fact, they took great pains to hide their bad habits from the coach's watchful eyes.

Buckingham Palace, It Wasn't

Shortly after she was hired as a full-time teacher and part-time coach of the women's basketball team at Tennessee, Joan Cronan and her husband, Tom, decided to visit the Knoxville campus. Joan was especially interested in locating the building where her team would play its home basketball games. After several trips around the campus, however, she was befuddled.

"I thought Tennessee was a beautiful place but I kept thinking, 'Where's the gym?'" she recalled. "I figured I was going to spend a good bit of my life there, so I wanted to know where it was."

Eventually, she stopped and asked for directions to Alumni Memorial Gymnasium. Finally locating the building, she was less than thrilled by the ancient facility's appearance. "We kept driving past this building that looked like a castle," she said. "It turned out that was the gym."

"We drove our own cars on road trips, and I remember us lagging behind Joan's car, so we could smoke cigarettes," Hill said. "We'd hold the cigarettes out the window, and we always lagged behind so Joan wouldn't catch us."

Like their cigarettes, the Volettes' games were a well-kept secret. Knoxville's two daily newspapers ignored the team, as did most of the university's students. The only incentive to play was love of the game.

"There was no fan support," Hill said. "We were lucky if we got a crowd of twenty people at our games. It just wasn't that big a deal. There was not a whole lot of interest generated by women's athletics at that time. We enjoyed the game but we certainly didn't play for an audience."

Cronan hoped to beef up the crowds, but first she wanted to beef up Tennessee's schedule. Upon assuming the reins from Nancy Lay in 1968, the new coach immediately set about lining up more games against better opposition. "Nancy's team had played three or four games the year before, so I wanted to increase our schedule," Cronan recalled. "I remember telling someone, 'Someday, we'll have a state tournament for women's basketball.' That's how far we were thinking ahead."

A more immediate concern was molding a rover team out of girls who had played half-court basketball in high school. That would be a real learning experience—not only for Tennessee's players but also for Tennessee's coach. Cronan had coached half-court basketball at Northwestern Louisiana, so she would be learning the nuances of rover ball while teaching them to her players.

"Trying to teach somebody how to play offense in six months wasn't going to work," she said. "We had to take mostly forwards [offensive players] from the six-player game. It's easier to teach defense than offense, and I've always been an offense-minded coach."

Cronan wasn't sure she could make her troops perform like basketball players, but she was determined to make them *look* like basketball players. "The team had been playing in T-shirts and shorts when I got there," she recalled. "I wanted to order uniforms, take us to the next level."

Unfortunately, few manufacturers were making women's basketball attire at the time, and none of those that did offered

*"Jump-shot Jane" Hill liter-
ally took scoring to new
heights at Tennessee.*
Bill Tracy Photography

More than a Pretty Face

During her two years as women's basketball coach at Tennessee, Joan Cronan realized that men's coach Ray Mears was a no-nonsense guy and that assistant coach Stu Aberdeen was even more so. So she was understandably rattled when Aberdeen showed up at her office door one day.

"May I help you?" she asked, hoping the nervousness in her voice was not too noticeable.

Aberdeen paused, and Cronan felt herself growing increasingly tense. But when the Vol aide finally spoke, she could feel the tension rushing from her body like a tidal wave. "One of our players, Mary Dell Hibler, was a very attractive blonde," Cronan recalled years later. "Stu just wanted to ask if the basketball staff could use her as a hostess for recruiting visits."

Joan gave her blessing—provided, of course, Miss Hibler agreed. As Aberdeen left the office, Cronan breathed a sigh of relief. All of her subsequent dealings with both Mears and Aberdeen would prove most cordial.

"Ray Mears was real cooperative," she said. "We worked together, and I never had any trouble with him—but I was smart enough not to push it too far."

orange uniforms. Cronan eventually found white uniforms with orange lettering for road games. Since home teams were not supposed to wear white, and orange was not available, the coach was forced to find another color for the home uniforms. "I had to decide what color went well with orange lettering," she said. "I liked Carolina blue, so that's where the Lady Vol colors came in."

Within a few years manufacturers began stocking orange uniforms. By then, however, Carolina blue had become ingrained in the Lady Vol tradition. To this day, UT's women athletes always have at least a hint of Carolina blue on their uniforms.

Once she had acquired uniforms, Cronan set about acquiring some support. She was pleasantly surprised to learn that school administrators were actually interested in her program. "It was important to Tennessee that we do well," she said. "Even though I was teaching full-time and getting just $500 per year to coach the team and another $500 for expenses, I felt there was a commitment to women's athletics."

Most schools exhibited no commitment to women's sports until 1976, when Title IX legislation forced them to provide equal opportunities for women. By then, Tennessee was well on its way to building a dynasty. Cronan put it best: "Before it was the law, before it was a cool thing to say you cared about women's athletics, this place actually cared."

Another pleasant surprise awaiting the new coach was a couple of outstanding players: Jane Hill of Dandridge and Anne Sprouse of Knoxville. "Anne was one of the purest shooters I ever coached, but she couldn't play a lick of defense," Cronan remembered. "And I called Jane Hill 'Jump-Shot Jane' because she was the first girl I'd ever seen shoot a jump shot.

"Richard Head [father of current Lady Vol coach Pat Head Summitt] likes to say, 'Don't bring donkeys to the Kentucky Derby.' Well, we had a couple of real thoroughbreds back then who would still be outstanding even in today's game."

At age twenty-three, Cronan was basically an older sister to the players on that 1968–69 team. Sensing they might try to challenge her authority, the coach became a little more aloof and businesslike than she might've been otherwise. "I was two years older than the players in those days, but they tell me now they thought I was a lot older than I really was back then," she said with a laugh. "It was a case of 'fake it till you make it,' I guess."

In Hill, Sprouse, and Knoxville natives Jan Jardet and Billie Anderton, Tennessee seemed to have excellent scoring potential. "We weren't a bad offensive team," Cronan said. "I think I was a pretty good offensive coach, but I'm not sure I was a good defensive coach at all."

That concern probably deepened when she opened her Tennessee career with a 77–46 loss at Western Carolina. The Volettes bounced back five days later, however, to upset powerful Tennessee Tech 45–43 in the home opener. That victory started a streak that saw them prevail in six of seven games, the lone loss coming in a home-floor rematch with Western Carolina.

School documents indicate Cronan finished her debut season on The Hill with an 8–4 record, omitting the team's participation in the season-ending Tennessee Tech Invitational. Cronan is happy to fill in the blanks. "We reached the finals of the Tennessee Tech tournament, then lost to Tech in a really close game right at the end," she said. "I remember that being a very disappointing loss. I guess that shows how competitive I am that I remember the losses, not the wins."

Ex-coach Joan Cronan
now serves as women's
athletic director.
Randy Moore/Rocky Top News

Is That You, Mom?

Joan Cronan had been entrusted with overseeing impression-able young women during her days as head coach of the Tennessee women's basketball program in 1968–69 and 1969–70. That was a picnic, however, compared to the task she faced as women's athletics director in March 1991.

With the Lady Vols preparing to play in the Final Four at New Orleans, Cronan was designated to serve as chaperone during the team's tour of the Big Easy. Naturally, the players eventually made their way to Bourbon Street. Naturally, they peeked in the door of a strip club just in time to see a young girl doing the old bump-and-grind. Cronan felt compelled to express her displeasure.

"That's somebody's daughter," she grumbled, sounding suitably indignant.

As the players continued down New Orleans's most famous street, they passed another strip joint. Again peering inside, they saw Lily St. Clair, whose career as a stripper had begun long before any of the Lady Vols were born.

Hoping to expand on Cronan's earlier comment, Debbie Hawhee gushed, "My goodness! That's somebody's mother!"

All things considered, though, that 1968–69 season was a rousing success. "We were a sports club and we knew that role," Cronan said. "Still, I got the feeling Tennessee could be a leader. I think we were all excited just to have the opportunity to compete. That was really the foundation as we went forward."

The biggest disappointments of that first year were the lack of support from the students and the lack of coverage from the Knoxville-area newspapers and television stations. "Student support wasn't much," Cronan recalled, "and the media coverage was awful. You'd get one line: 'And the Volettes won.' I saw the coverage the guys were getting and thought, 'If we can do this for men, why not for women?'"

A year later, Cronan resigned as head coach and cut back to part-time teaching in order to devote herself to starting a family. Her coaching days at Tennessee were finished, but she would return to the school eleven years later as women's athletics director.

Although the administration had been generally supportive during her two-year stint as Tennessee's head coach, Cronan was mildly disappointed that the Lady Vols continued to play in 3,000-seat Alumni Gym while the men's basketball team played in 12,700-seat Stokely Athletics Center. If her players felt slighted, however, they never expressed it.

"We played in a very old gymnasium, but we didn't consider that an obstacle," Hill recalled. "And we had a wonderful time on road trips."

Especially when their smoke-filled cars were beyond the range of Cronan's rearview mirror.

It All Began with a Bluff

Shortly after addressing a motley crew of sixty walk-on candidates for the University of Tennessee women's basketball team, first-year coach Margaret Hutson headed for the Alumni Gym exit, grateful that no one had discovered her embarrassing little secret. She was nearly out the door when a soft voice stopped her in her tracks.

"Coach, are we going to play pattern or freelance?"

Hutson took a deep breath, buying some time while waiting for her mind to kick into overdrive. Finally, she turned to face the speaker.

"I had no idea what the young lady was asking," Hutson recalled years later.

That's because the thirty-two-year-old instructor knew almost nothing about basketball. Except for participating in a few church league outings and overseeing a loosely organized prep school team, she was a virtual stranger to the game she now was preparing to coach.

Hutson knew her options were limited. She could: A) admit her relative ignorance of the sport, or B) try to bluff her way through. Within a matter of seconds, she decided the second option was a whole lot more palatable. "I suppose," she said, measuring her words carefully, "it will depend on what our personnel will be."

Satisfied with the purposely vague response, the player nodded, then turned to leave.

Heart pounding, the coach breathed a sigh of relief as she made her way through the door and outside into the cool October evening.

In those day's the university's administration didn't view Hutson's lack of a hoops background as significant—largely because women's basketball wasn't viewed as significant. As a glorified club sport, it had virtually no funding, no fan base, and no publicity. In short, it was the best-kept secret on campus. To illustrate: Hutson's hiring as a UT physical education instructor closed with the after-thought: "By the way, you'll be coaching women's basketball."

One less-than-enthusiastic "okay" later, Margaret Hutson found herself in charge of the women's basketball program at a major university. No press conference. No contract. Not even a handshake. The job was so incidental it just didn't seem worth the bother.

"That's the way it was done back then," Hutson said. "You were a teacher in the physical education department *and* you coached. I had reservations about the basketball, but I was young and idealistic."

She was beyond idealistic. She was living in a fantasyland.

"Somebody told me that Yale's swimming coach won national titles even though he couldn't swim himself," she mused. "I kept thinking about that and saying, 'I can do this.'"

Incredibly, she was right. Her fourth Tennessee team won twenty-five of twenty-seven games and made a pretty strong run at the national championship. But the road to that glorious achievement was a long and winding one.

Hutson had never played competitive basketball, but she had come close once. A native East Tennessean, she had planned to try out for the girls team at Chattanooga High School in the mid-1950s, but an injury prevented her from doing so. After taking her undergraduate degree from Tennessee–Chattanooga in 1960, she directed a girls basketball team at Greer Preparatory School in Tyrone, Pennsylvania, completed her master's degree at North Carolina–Greensboro, and then helped coach the women's basketball team at Shippensburg (Pennsylvania) State College.

She returned to her home state and was working for Chattanooga's public school system in 1970 when the desire to teach at a large university prompted her to apply for work at the University of Tennessee–Knoxville. She was surprised to land a job. She was even more surprised to learn the job also entailed coaching women's basketball. Being a resilient sort, however, she embarked on a crash course to learn the game's basics. She read books on the subject. She picked the brain of Stu Aberdeen, assistant coach for the Tennessee men's team. She attended camp after camp after camp, one of which was located in Greensboro, North Carolina, and featured college players serving as counselors. Among the counselors was an ultra-intense University of Tennessee–Martin player named Pat Head, the woman who eventually would become Hutson's successor at UT. Small world.

While developing a working knowledge of the game, Hutson set about securing some talent. She posted flyers all over campus seeking young women who could shoot, rebound, or defend. Finding anyone with more than one of these skills would be a bonus. The coach had no idea what to expect when she showed up for her first meeting with the raw recruits. She was pleasantly surprised by the quantity, if not the quality. "Sixty showed up," she recalled. "It was remarkable."

Because Tennessee high schools were still playing the outdated six-girl, half-court game, most of Hutson's prospects had played offense or defense, but not both. To help them learn to make the transition from defense to offense—and vice versa—she staged a miniclinic featuring Jimmy England, star guard for the campus men's team.

Now that she had some know-how and some players, Hutson's final task was to locate some funding. To raise money for travel and a host of miscellaneous expenses, the team held an assortment of fund-raisers, including doughnut sales. The team even traveled to Sunbright to play an exhibition game against the local boys' high school team. The take was only $200, but, as Hutson noted, "It helped."

There were still few manufacturers making women's basketball uniforms at the time, and none making them in orange, so Hutson's troops continued to wear the blue uniforms with orange lettering adopted by predecessor Joan Cronan. It would be Hutson's fourth season at the helm before her team donned orange attire.

The women's basketball program was getting scant attention from the local newspapers, the *Knoxville Journal* and *Knoxville News-Sentinel*, but that was probably just as well. Both papers still referred to the team as the Volettes, a nickname that Hutson found less than desirable. "We just called ourselves Tennessee Women's Basketball," she recalled.

Lacking a reasonable travel budget, the team played almost all of its games within a 150-mile radius of Knoxville. This filled the schedule with assorted small colleges such as Carson-Newman, Milligan, Middle Tennessee State, Western Carolina, and Tennessee–Chattanooga. Players and coaches traveled to road games in vans. Still, this represented an upgrade; previously, staffers and athletes had driven to away games in their personal cars, powered by gas bought with money from their own pockets. This was the ultimate in no-frills competition.

Hutson's first team featured just one player who stood more than 6 feet tall: 6'1" guard Gloria Scott, who had been an all-state defensive player at Bradley County High School. Though they were small in stature, the Volettes had plenty of speed and spunk. They also had a lot of stamina. That was fortunate, considering the demands placed on their youthful bodies. "They had to be in shape because we would go to tournaments and play two or three games in *one* day," Hutson said. "Plus, we played a fast-break offense and man-to-man defense, so conditioning was crucial."

Indeed. Near the conclusion of Hutson's first season, Tennessee hosted the Tennessee Collegiate Women's Sports Federation's eastern district tournament. The host team lost 53–47 to Chattanooga on the morning of February 26 but came back later in the day to beat Carson-Newman 52–37. Tennessee played twice more the following day, beating Milligan and East Tennessee State University. Three wins and a loss in forty-eight hours is a lot of basketball, especially for young women who were considered too fragile to play full-court at the high school level.

"We ran an awful lot in practice," Hutson remembered. "You had to do that when you were playing two or three games in a day."

That 1970–71 team lost twice in the state tournament at Memphis to finish with a modest 6–6 record. Still, it was a group of young women Hutson will never forget. "The main thing I remember," she said, "is what great competitors they were and how hard they worked."

With Hutson developing rapidly as a coach, Tennessee improved dramatically the next year. The 1971–72 team opened by dumping Middle Tennessee State 55–45, then followed with a 35–29 defeat of the Maryville All-Stars, a 51–45 defeat of Carson-Newman, and a 72–26 road win at Milligan. A 78–56 drubbing of East Tennessee State improved Tennessee's record to 5–0, but the Volettes were just getting started. They clipped Tennessee–Chattanooga 58–48, Cumberland 52–35, Carson-Newman 71–41, South Carolina 44–30, and Western Carolina 48–44 to complete a sizzling 10–0 start.

Inexplicably, the team's fortunes took a downward turn at this point. Playing mere hours after its defeat of Western Carolina, leg-weary Tennessee lost 51–36 to North Carolina–Greensboro. Their perfect season shattered, the Volettes lost four of their remaining seven games to finish 13–5. Still, this represented a vast improvement over the 6–6 mark of the previous season.

Hutson's third year brought another hot start and another step up in class. The 1972–73 team won twelve of its first fourteen games, including the program's first-ever TCWSF eastern district title. Playing in Johnson City, the Volettes beat Maryville (69–57), Carson-Newman (56–50), and Tennessee–Chattanooga (55–51)— all within forty-eight hours—to claim the championship.

Playing in the TCWSF state tournament at Maryville, Tennessee opened with a 58–43 drubbing of Middle Tennessee State, then came back later that day to beat Tennessee–Martin 59–57 in overtime. Martin's star player, Pat Head, launched a potential game-tying shot from half-court at the final buzzer.

"It was like slow-motion," Hutson recalled. "It went up and up and then came down, hit the rim and came out. Pat was such a competitor that, as a coach, I felt sad her team didn't get to go on. I went over to talk with her after the game, and she was very disappointed."

Tennessee lost a 48–45 heartbreaker to powerhouse Tennessee Tech in the tourney semifinals but bounced back in the consolation round to beat Martin in overtime again, this time by a 61–57 score. Boasting a 15–3 record, the Volettes then accepted the first bid in program history to the Association of Intercollegiate Athletics for Women (AIAW) tournament. This was the female equivalent of a men's team getting a bid to the National Collegiate Athletics Association championships. Tennessee was assigned to the Region II tournament at Lexington, Kentucky.

Helping Tennessee post a 25–2 record in 1973–74 were (left to right) Joy Scruggs, Gail Dobson Ingram, coach Margaret Hutson, Gloria Scott Deathridge, and Nancy Bowman Ladd. Photo courtesy Knoxville News-Sentinel

Tennessee trounced Longwood 61–43 in the Region II opener at Lexington, Kentucky, but fell 59–54 to South Carolina in Round 2. Unable to bounce back from the disappointment, the Volettes dropped the third-place game to Tennessee Tech 61–48 later that evening. Still, a 16–5 record and a first-ever bid to the national tournament suggested Hutson's program was on the fast track to the big-time. "We were very pleased to qualify for that tournament," Hutson recalled. "Even with Lexington being close by, it was a big deal."

Another big deal occurred in 1973–74, when Hutson finally gained an assistant coach. Former Austin Peay player Pam Davidson, pursuing her master's at Tennessee, agreed to help oversee the program. Even so, there was nothing in Tennessee's opener to suggest Hutson's fourth season would be anything special. The homestanding Volettes struggled mightily before subduing Marshall 44–40.

Then a funny thing happened: The team jelled into a juggernaut. Tennessee won its next ten outings by an average of 25 points, boosting its record to 11–0. Though pleased, Hutson remained cautious. After all, her 1971–72 team had opened 10–0, only to lose five of its last eight games. Besides, the Volettes were about to step up in class. Game 12 would bring them face-to-face with Marynell Meadors' powerful Tennessee Tech squad. Moreover, the game was to be played before a hostile crowd in Cookeville.

Proving themselves capable of going toe-to-toe with the best in the women's game, the Volettes hammered Tech 65–51, moving to 12–0 and finally gaining the attention of the Knoxville media. Newspapers began running stories on their games. Television stations recapped their exploits during the sports highlights.

Meanwhile, Tennessee's players continued to provide plenty of exploits. They concluded the regular season 17–0, with the only single-digit victory margin having come in the opener against Marshall. Tennessee swept past Carson-Newman (59–41) and East Tennessee State (54–41) to win the TCWSF eastern district title, then beat Austin Peay in Round 1 of the TCWSF state tourney, improving its record to 20–0.

Through it all, the head coach remained remarkably calm. The team trainer—if Tennessee had one—would've been tempted to check Hutson's pulse occasionally, just to make sure she was still alive. "I just sat on the bench," she recalled. "That's just my personality. Everybody's different and everybody reaches players in different ways. I never jumped up and down. I *could* give dirty looks, though."

Given her low-key personality, Hutson drew just one technical foul during her entire Tennessee tenure—and it was related to injury, not insult. As one of her players was writhing in pain on the floor, the head coach/trainer rushed onto the court to lend assistance. In her haste to reach the fallen player, she had not waited to be recognized by the referee, thus incurring a technical foul—and an apology. "Right before she gave me the technical, the ref came over and said, 'Margaret, I hate to do this to you because you never give us any trouble.'"

As the Volettes' record soared, so did their popularity. Television sportscasters began giving their scores on a regular basis. Newspaper reporters suddenly found their way to the gym. A Knoxville civic club asked Hutson to address its members. Still, the team continued playing in tiny Alumni Gym, while the Tennessee men played in 12,700-seat Stokely Athletics Center. "The closest we ever got to playing in Stokely Center," Hutson recalled wistfully, "is when we were 20–0 and got an introduction at halftime of a men's game."

A 57–50 defeat of Memphis State moved Tennessee to 21–0 and into the TCWSF state finals. But Tennessee Tech, playing on its home floor in Cookeville, dealt the Volettes their first setback of the season, winning a 54–51 overtime thriller. Tennessee bounced back later that day to trip Memphis State 52–41, capturing second place and a second consecutive bid to

The Original "Wrap" Star

Modern coaches spend a lot of time with tape—videotape, that is. Back in the early days of Tennessee women's basketball, though, coach Margaret Hutson spent some time with another kind of tape—the medical kind.

Because there was no money in the Volettes' budget for a trainer, Hutson found herself in quite a quandary in the 1972 Tennessee Collegiate Women's Sports Federation tournament. In the late stages of a particularly hotly contested game, one of Tennessee's players came limping to the bench with a sprained ankle. With no one else to do the job, Hutson knelt beside the injured player, then angled her body so she could monitor the action on the playing floor. She'd apply a strip of tape, then grab a quick glance at the action. Another strip of tape . . . another glance. And so it went. "I was trying to tape her ankle and coach at the same time," Hutson recalled.

The game might have ended before the coach's wrapping job did, if not for a kindly woman in the stands. Making her way through the crowd, the woman arrived at Tennessee's bench and offered Hutson a lifeline. "Here, let me do that, Margaret," the Good Samaritan said. "You coach."

Hutson still smiles at the recollection.

"Those were the days."

the AIAW Tournament. The next stop would be the Region II tourney at Harrisonburg, Virginia.

Since the Volettes had brought the university considerable positive publicity, Hutson thought her players deserved a little something in return. Specifically, she wanted the school to charter a bus, so her players wouldn't have to endure the long drive to Harrisonburg in vans. After some initial resistance, school brass agreed to the request.

Shortly after completing the long trek, Tennessee found itself facing double duty on March 8. After mauling Madison 74–43, the Volettes routed Roanoke 68–47. Their weary legs failed them on Day 2, however, and they suffered a 55–53 loss to Winthrop. Showing tremendous resilience, they came back later in the day to trounce Western Carolina 66–51 for third place. Tennessee didn't make the Final Four, but its 25–2 record indicated the program was now on par with the country's best.

"That was a very strong team for its time," Hutson remembered. "Sometimes you get kids who are good athletes with no work ethic. Those kids had talent *and* work ethic. That was the winning combination right there."

Even with Tennessee coming off the greatest season in program history, Hutson decided she'd had enough. She informed university officials she was stepping down as coach in order to attend some graduate classes. Though eager to teach one more year, she insisted her basketball days were finished. Amazingly, she kept that vow, walking away from the game and never coaching it again.

The university quickly filled the void in its hoops program by hiring Pat Head, who was finishing up her senior year at UT–Martin and shopping for a suitable master's program. She

Joy Scruggs (left), Gail Dobson Ingram, Gloria Scott Deathridge, and coach Margaret Hutson (right) of the 1973–74 Volettes held a mini-reunion in 1997.
Emory & Henry Sports Information file photo

eventually became Pat Head Summitt, the dominant coach in women's basketball—leading Tennessee to six national titles during the 1980s and 1990s. Hutson, meanwhile, became a trivia answer—literally. A game based on Tennessee trivia was marketed in the 1990s, and one of the questions asked players to name Summitt's predecessor. Upon seeing the trivia card, Hutson couldn't stifle a chuckle.

"If they ever do a second edition," she quipped, "maybe they can spell my name with a T instead of a D."

The Farmer's Daughter

It was a typical autumn afternoon in the sleepy West Tennessee town of Henrietta. With most grownups working in the fields or at the few downtown businesses, the streets were almost deserted. The quiet calm of the area was disrupted only by the buzz of excitement and shrieks of laughter emanating from the Fredonia Elementary School playground.

Among the children enjoying recess was Trish Head, so tall and thin classmates teasingly called her "Bone" or, worse, "Bonehead." The comments stung a bit, but the soft-spoken country girl never responded to them—never even acknowledged them. She just retreated a little deeper into her bashful nature and wondered why she couldn't be short like the other girls. What good was height, anyway?

The answer was forthcoming. Leisurely popping up and down on a playground seesaw, Trish was totally immersed in the activity when the school principal's voice boomed out above the playground noise. "Trish! Trish Head! Come over here a minute."

"What have I done now?" she thought, bouncing off the seesaw as soon as her feet touched ground.

Unsure what to expect, her pace slowed and her pulse quickened as she approached the principal. To her surprise, his expression was pleasant, not stern. "You're tall for a girl," he began. "Except for one boy, you're probably the tallest student in your class. Would you be interested in playing basketball?"

Trish paused thoughtfully, then gave a tentative nod that would dramatically alter the course of women's athletics—not only in Henrietta, but around the world.

Six years later she enrolled at the University of Tennessee–Martin, where, despite an abiding love for history, she would major in physical education while honing her basketball skills. Her destiny was not to study history, but to *make* it.

Clearly, she has fulfilled that destiny. Trish Head became Pat Head Summitt; the backward preteen known as "Bone" became known as the premier coach in the game. On March 22, 2005, she notched her 880th career victory, eclipsing legendary North Carolina men's coach Dean Smith to become the biggest winner in the history of college basketball.

Before she could enjoy resounding victories, however, she had to endure a devastating setback. Four games into her senior year at Martin, she tore the anterior cruciate ligament in her left knee. The injury caused her to miss the rest of the 1973–74 season and placed her career in jeopardy. "Forget it," a somber-faced surgeon told her, certain she would never play again. Undeterred, Head accepted an offer from the University of Tennessee that would allow her to teach some classes and coach women's basketball while pursuing her master's degree.

The offer could be traced to Nancy Lay, who had coached women's hoops at UT during the 1960s and returned to the school as coordinator of women's athletics in 1973. Assuming this "marvelous player" had the traits needed to become a quality coach, Lay recommended Head to Helen B. Watson, overseer of Tennessee's physical education department. Watson offered the job, and Head accepted after mulling a similar offer from Memphis State University.

Months later twenty-two-year-old Pat Head guided the 1974–75 Volettes to a 16–8 record. Shortly after her second season produced an equally uninspiring 16–11 mark, she showed up for the U.S. Olympic basketball trials with a surgically repaired knee and more hope than optimism.

Because the injury and subsequent weight gain had robbed her of some quickness and mobility, Head suspected she might be a longshot to make the Olympic team. That suspicion was confirmed shortly before the U.S. team trials by head coach

Billie Moore. "You need to lose ten to fifteen pounds," the coach said, "and be in the best shape of your life to make this team."

Head lost twenty-seven pounds, won a spot on the Olympic team, served as co-captain, and helped guide the squad to a silver medal at the '76 Montreal Games. Then she returned to Knoxville and, in just her third year as a head coach, guided the 1976–77 Lady Vols to a 28–5 record and a third-place finish in the Association of Intercollegiate Athletics for Women Final Four.

Her 1977–78 team achieved a 27–2 record and a number-one national ranking before suffering an upset loss to Maryland in AIAW regional play. She posted the first thirty-win season in school history the next year, when her Lady Vols made the Final Four but lost to Louisiana Tech in the semifinal round. She inched the team one step closer to the title in 1979–80, when the Lady Vols reached the national title game before falling to Old Dominion. The next year she changed her marital status and her name—becoming Pat Head Summitt—but she couldn't change her luck. Tennessee reached the title game and then lost to Louisiana Tech.

The NCAA supplanted the AIAW as the governing body for women's basketball in 1981–82, but Summitt's Final Four futility continued. She guided Tennessee to the national semifinals in 1982, the finals in 1984, and the semifinals in 1986, but each season ended with a loss. Seven times she'd been to the Big Dance. Seven times she'd fallen short of the Big Prize. "Before 1987, I felt like I was bluffing," she recalled years later.

Though haunted by those Final Four disappointments, Summitt's consolation prize was pretty impressive: She coached

Pat Head was a fresh-faced twenty-two-year-old when she began her coaching career. University of Tennessee Photography Center

You're in Pat's Army Now

Candidates for the University of Tennessee women's basketball team showed up for the first preseason practice of 1974–75 expecting to meet their new coach. Instead, they met a drill sergeant in sneakers.

Pat Head, twenty-two, was only a year older than some of her players, so she wanted to establish from day one that she was in complete command. Besides, her father had been a taskmaster, so it was the leadership style she knew best.

Being a perfectionist carries a price, however, and the rookie coach learned as much in her early days with the Lady Vols. Her strenuous workouts and biting comments reduced some players to tears. Many transferred. Many more just quit. Even those who stayed felt isolated from the high-strung coach with the stern disposition.

"In the early years two vans would come to the airport to pick us up after games," she conceded in her autobiography, *Reach for the Summitt.* "The players would ride home in one, and I would ride with the equipment in the other."

Proving she could change with the times, Summitt gradually mellowed with experience. Although she remains a demanding coach, she no longer comes across as a lipstick-wearing pit bull. In retrospect, she realizes she has changed for the better.

"I really thought there were a lot of teams in the younger years that, had they had a more experienced coach, they might have won championships before we actually won in 1987," she said. "I would have had better teams, but also better relationships with the players. . . .

"I always heard you can start out tough and let up, but if you start out soft you may never get the results you need. I was probably too tough in those early years of my coaching and didn't take time to really get to know the players."

the U.S. women to a gold medal in the 1984 Olympic Games.

Still, success on the international stage couldn't negate the frustration she felt on the national level. So, upon reaching the NCAA finals again in 1987, she decided to change her strategy. Rather than send her players through the usual game-day morning workout, she ordered them to sit in a circle, eyes closed, and imagine every possible situation they might encounter in the title game later that evening.

"It worked," she recalled. "Our team came out and played like they had ESP." In this case, ESP must have stood for Extreme Summitt Personality. The Lady Vols were never more focused and driven as they crushed Louisiana Tech 67–44 to win the program's first-ever national title.

Summitt enjoyed her first championship so much she won another one in 1989 (beating Auburn 76–60 in the title game) and another in 1991 (nipping Virginia 70–67 in overtime for the crown). Then the ultrasuccessful coach hit the only real "slump" of her career. Between 1992 and 1994, she missed the Final Four three years in a row—a feat unprecedented in her twenty-year career. She returned to the Big Dance in 1995 but lost to Connecticut in the title game. After claiming three national championships in the six-year span from 1987 to 1991, Summitt found herself in a four-year drought. "The women's game has caught up with Tennessee," critics proclaimed.

Summitt made no reply, just as she had made no reply when classmates back in Henrietta called her "Bonehead." It simply wasn't her style. Instead, she went out and won unprecedented back-to-back-to-back NCAA titles in 1996, 1997, and 1998. With six national titles in twelve years, Summitt made her point without saying a word: The women's game hadn't caught up with Tennessee just yet.

Although the Lady Vols haven't won a national title since 1998, they haven't exactly disappeared—posting four runner-up finishes between 1999 and 2004. They continue to be the program against which all others are measured. And Pat Summitt continues to be the coach against whom all others are measured.

Her winning formula is no secret. It was instilled in her childhood and ingrained in her coaching philosophy: "It is much more difficult to handle success than failure," she said. "At the top, there are no days off."

Working longer, harder, and more productively than her rivals has enabled Summitt to build a program that serves as the national model for success. Of course, success is a relative term. At Tennessee, it means thirty-plus victories, Southeastern Conference regular-season and tournament titles, followed by a national championship. Anything less is considered a rebuilding year.

Sometimes, though, even a national title isn't enough. Lacking the discipline and toughness of most Summitt-coached squads, the 1996–97 team did not meet the coach's lofty standards. As the players continued losing games, Summitt continued losing her patience. A 17-point home-floor loss to Stanford on December 15 was humiliating. Consecutive double-digit losses to Connecticut (72–57) and Old Dominion (83–72) in early January dropped the Lady Vols' record to a dismal 9–7. The team rallied briefly but then lost its final two regular-season games—dropping the finale at Louisiana Tech by 18 points.

After an unthinkable fifth-place finish in Southeastern Conference play, Tennessee hoped to redeem itself in the league tournament. Instead, the Lady Vols bowed to Auburn 61–59 and saw their record sink to 23–10. By Summitt standards, that amounted to a losing season. The fact Tennessee ranked tenth in the Associated Press national poll was more a testament to the coach's will than to her team's skill.

Relying on vigilance more than optimism, Summitt kept pushing her team, kept molding her team, kept challenging her team. Finally, as March arrived, the troops responded. The Lady Vols won two NCAA subregional games on their home floor, then beat Colorado to reach the Midwest Region finals against top-ranked Connecticut. Then, in one of the greatest upsets ever recorded, a ten-loss Tennessee team stunned the Huskies 91–81 to earn a bid to the Final Four in Cincinnati. The Cinderella story concluded a week later with a 68–59 upset of Old Dominion in the title game and the most unlikely national championship in the history of women's hoops.

As the euphoria of another title subsided, however, Summitt pondered retirement. The 1996–97 team had confounded her, frustrated her, drained her. Losing was tolerable — barely — but playing uninspired, undisciplined basketball was not.

"When we were going through that, I wasn't sure I was going to do this much longer," she later admitted. "I don't handle losing well at all. But it was more about coaching players who didn't give it their all. I don't like coaching effort. I'm not good at it, and you don't want me to try to be good at it."

Instead of changing vocations, Summitt decided to change her recruiting methods. She began focusing as much on a player's mental makeup as her basketball skills. There would be no more slackers in her program. "Tennessee is not for every-

Pat Head Summitt's Milestones

- **December 7, 1974:** Pat Head loses 84–83 to Mercer in her first game as a college coach.

- **January 10, 1975:** Head defeats Middle Tennessee State 69–32 for her first college victory.

- **November 13, 1976:** Head's Lady Vols (previously known as the Volettes) move from 3,200-seat Alumni Gym to 12,700-seat Stokely Athletics Center and enjoy a smashing debut. Trish Roberts scores a school-record 51 points in a 107–53 thrashing of Kentucky.

- **January 13, 1979:** Tennessee beats North Carolina State 79–66 at Raleigh for Head's one hundredth victory.

- **November 28, 1980:** Now married, Pat Head Summitt opens her seventh season with a 74–62 defeat of Alabama.

- **December 3, 1982:** Summitt's team defeats St. John's 69–56 for victory number 200.

- **January 4, 1987:** Tennessee beats North Carolina 87–68, giving its coach win number 300.

- **March 29, 1987:** The Lady Vols beat Louisiana Tech 67–44 at Austin, Texas, for the first national title in program history.

- **December 3, 1987:** Tennessee trounces Stetson 102–59 in its first regular-season game at Thompson-Boling Arena.

- **April 2, 1989:** The Lady Vols beat Auburn 76–70 at Tacoma, Washington, for their second NCAA title in three years.

- **January 25, 1990:** Tennessee nips South Carolina 70–69 in Columbia, giving Summitt win number 400.

- March 31, 1991: The Lady Vols edge Virginia 70–67 in overtime at New Orleans for their third national title in five years.

- November 21, 1993: Summitt notches victory number 500 as Tennessee prevails 80–45 against Ohio State, coached by former Summitt aide Nancy Darsch. The game is played in Jackson, Tennessee, as part of the State Farm Hall of Fame Tip-Off Classic.

- March 31, 1996: Summitt posts national title number four by beating Georgia 83–65 at Charlotte.

- November 23, 1996: Victory number 600 for Summitt is an 83–68 defeat of Marquette in the Howard Bank Classic at Burlington, Vermont.

- March 30, 1997: Tennessee beats Old Dominion 68–59 at Cincinnati for its second national championship in a row and fifth overall.

- February 22, 1998: The Lady Vols beat Louisiana State University 90–58, improving to 30–0 and concluding the first unbeaten regular season in program history.

- March 29, 1998: Tennessee trounces Louisiana Tech 93–75 at Kansas City to cap an unprecedented 39–0 season and an equally unprecedented third consecutive NCAA title.

- January 17, 1999: More than fifty former Lady Vols show up at Thompson-Boling Arena to celebrate Summitt's silver anniversary as coach. Tennessee thrashes Kentucky 98–60.

- June, 1999: Summitt is inducted into the Women's Basketball Hall of Fame.

(continued)

- December 5, 1999: Summitt becomes the second women's coach to win 700 games (Texas's Jody Conradt was the first) as Tennessee clips Wisconsin 85–62 at Madison.

- March 5, 2000: The Lady Vols beat Mississippi State 70–67 in Chattanooga to win their third consecutive Southeastern Conference tournament title.

- April 2000: Summitt is named Naismith Coach of the Century.

- October 13, 2000: Summitt is inducted into Naismith Basketball Hall of Fame.

- January 14, 2003: Tennessee beats DePaul 76–57 at Thompson-Boling Arena, making Summitt the first women's coach to reach the 800-victory plateau.

- March 22, 2005: Tennessee defeats Purdue 75–54 in NCAA Tournament second-round play at Thompson-Boling Arena for Summitt's 880th win. The victory breaks a tie with former University of North Carolina men's coach Dean Smith and makes Summitt the winningest coach in the history of college basketball.

- March 29, 2005: Tennessee beats Rutgers 59–49 in the NCAA East Region finals, giving Summitt her sixteenth Final Four bid. Former UCLA men's coach John Wooden ranks second with twelve.

body," she told recruits. Those who weren't scared off by this warning had to undergo a screening process called the Predictive Index, a questionnaire that reveals an individual's competitiveness. Essentially, Summitt wanted to play God, creating a team in her own image—a roster stocked with players driven by success and tormented by failure.

She succeeded. Loaded with Type-A personalities, her 1997–98 team went 39–0, won by an average of 30 points per game, and captured the program's third consecutive national championship by trouncing Louisiana Tech 93–75 in the NCAA title game.

Because Tennessee produces so many All-Americans, there is a widespread perception that Summitt doesn't recruit—she selects. Fans and foes alike suspect she picks three or four prospects she deems most worthy each year, hands them scholarship papers, then signs off on recruiting until the following year. It isn't quite that simple, even for the queen of women's basketball.

"People think we can go out and select, but that's not true," she said. "We work hard in recruiting, but I tell them, 'If you want to be the showboat, go somewhere else. If you want to be on the showboat, then come to Tennessee.'"

In a profession where paranoia rules, Summitt is a remarkable exception. She shares her thoughts on preparing, motivating, and strategizing with anyone who attends one of her camps or one of her practices—even rival coaches. After all, knowing how to align Rubik's Cube doesn't ensure a person the discipline and determination to actually complete the task. Besides, Summitt figures sharing information ultimately elevates women's basketball to a higher level of excellence.

Ho-hum . . . another national title. Randy Moore/Rocky Top News

"I'm not afraid to share," she said. "I feel like I should do everything I can to help the game. When I share, I end up learning something new, as well. When you quit learning, you need to get out of it."

No story on this remarkable woman would be complete without a mention of some classic Summitt tales that have been retold so many times they now qualify as legend:

- In the early 1960s she spent countless hours in the hayloft, shooting baskets on a hoop her father, Richard Head, had mounted inside the family barn.

- In 1966, tears streaming down her cheeks, she missed her own sixteenth birthday party at the local country club because her dad insisted farm chores take precedence over social events. Yet this same super-strict father moved his family into another school district, just so his oldest daughter could attend a high school that offered girls' basketball.

- In 1978, after her top-ranked team lost an AIAW region semifinal game *and* the consolation game, she angrily loaded her players onto the team bus and insisted the eight-and-a-half-hour trek from Cleveland, Mississippi, to Knoxville be made with no stops for food or bathroom breaks.

- In 1980, arriving on campus in the wee hours after a second-half collapse at South Carolina, she ordered her players back into their sweaty uniforms and onto the practice floor. "Now you're going to go play the half you didn't play last night," she grumbled.

The Ultimate Challenge?

She drove a tractor as a teenager. She overcame a major knee injury that was supposed to end her basketball career. She won Olympic silver as a player and Olympic gold as a coach. She became a head coach without ever serving as an assistant. She started with a group of walk-ons and built the most dominating program in women's basketball. She won six national titles in twelve years. She recently won her 880th game, breaking the collegiate record set by North Carolina men's coach Dean Smith. She has single-handedly moved women's basketball ten years ahead of where it would be without her.

Is there a challenge too demanding for Pat Summitt? Apparently not. Given all she has accomplished, the ultimate challenge would seem to be remaining humble in the face of such remarkable achievements. Yet she has met this challenge, too.

"I've been called a pioneer, a trailblazer and a legend," she said recently. "All three make me feel old. I don't see myself as someone who did all of this alone. There have been thousands of women across America, long before Pat Summitt was coaching, who really tried to break ground for women, women's sports, in the corporate arena and in politics. A lot of doors have been opened. There's a different level of respect now and the opportunities are far greater than they've ever been for women to leave college and pursue their dreams."

- In the 1980s, upon learning her athletes had attended an all-night party the previous evening, she placed garbage cans at the four corners of the practice floor and ran the players until they vomited into them.

- In 1991 her water broke while she was visiting the home of Pennsylvania prospect Michelle Marciniak. On the emergency flight back home, Summitt refused to land in Virginia and give birth to her son in that state. The reason? The University of Virginia's Lady Cavaliers had upset Tennessee in the 1990 NCAA East Regional finals, costing Summitt a chance to play for the national title on the Lady Vols' home floor back in Knoxville.

- In 1994 she grabbed Marciniak's jersey as the player ran past and launched into an angry tirade because of a blown defensive assignment. A photo of the incident appeared on page 1 of Knoxville's daily newspaper the following morning with the caption: "Spinderella and her wicked stepmother."

- In the spring of 1994 she was asked to coach the university *men's* team following the ouster of head coach Wade Houston. Summitt declined. She got the same offer in 1997 (following the departure of Kevin O'Neill) and in 2001 (following the departure of Jerry Green) and gave the same response. "First, my commitment is to young women," she explained. "I also don't think coaching men is a step up."

- In 1995 she got her first-ever hug from her emotionally challenged father. Recuperating in her hotel room following a heartbreaking NCAA title game loss to Connecticut, she was shocked when Richard Head put his arms around her and muttered, "You've got nothing to be ashamed of. . . . I'm proud of you."

- In 1997 she was deeply moved when UT–Martin named its gym floor in her honor during pregame ceremonies. Still, she took no pity on her alma mater, guiding Tennessee to a 73–32 drubbing of the Skyhawks.

- In 1998 she graced the cover of *Sports Illustrated*, wearing "The Look," her infamous icy glare. Like her lanky frame, it is something she inherited from her father. "When Dad gave you that look, you knew you had better sit down and shut up," recalled Tommy Head, one of Pat's brothers. "And when you see Pat staring at the referees, you know where that came from. A lot of people are scared to death of her eyes."

Ah, yes . . . the eyes have it. Ask any official who has worked a Lady Vol game. Summitt's glare can intimidate even the most experienced veteran. So can the caustic barbs she tosses at them throughout the course of a game. She is particularly sharp-tongued when an opponent is being more physical than her team. "What are we playing today—football?" she'll snap. Or she'll shake her head at a passing official and mutter: "Are they using a hockey crew to run this game?"

No one—repeat, *no one*—works the officials better than Pat Summitt. Glaring and baiting are as much a part of her game-plan as Xs and Os. She will do anything within the rules that will help her win. Obviously, these tactics are effective. Her forty-year basketball odyssey has taken her from nobody to notoriety, producing as many ups and downs as that playground seesaw back at Fredonia Elementary School. The difference is, she'll finish this ride on top.

Once Summitt's ride truly is finished, she'll hang up her coaching whistle, nestle into an overstuffed chair, and immerse herself in a book on the Middle Ages. Or the Civil War. Or the Roaring Twenties. But that day hasn't arrived just yet.

There will be plenty of time to study history once she's through making it.

The
Secretary
of Defense

The home team was comfortably ahead, yet fans remained glued to their seats during the final minutes of Tennessee's 89–72 defeat of Clemson on February 18, 1980, at Stokely Athletics Center. Even after the final horn sounded, the vast majority remained seated, knowing the evening's festivities were not complete.

Their patience was rewarded moments later when Lady Vol athletics director Gloria

Ray stepped to midcourt, scanned the crowd, and smiled. Spectators grew hushed as Ray, a tiny lady with a big voice, began to speak. The message was simple: It was time to honor the greatest women's basketball player in university history by retiring her jersey number.

When a school retires a player's jersey, that's special recognition. When a school retires a player's jersey *before* the player's career concludes, that's reverence. Not one jersey had been retired in the eighty-nine-year history of varsity basketball at the University of Tennessee, but school officials felt compelled to break that tradition. They agreed it was time the university show some reverence for one of its own.

After a few opening remarks, Ray began describing the honoree in glowing terms ". . . a Knoxvillian, a true Tennessean, and an international ambassador for the United States. She is one of the finest walking definitions of the word 'All-American.' She is an All-American basketball player *and* an All-American person.

"There is no simple way to say thanks to someone who has meant so much to so many people," Ray continued, her voice choked with emotion. "But perhaps the most fitting way we can honor her is by joining with the coaches, players, and the women's athletics department as we retire number twenty-two, the jersey worn for four years by the Lady Vols' First Lady: Holly Warlick."

As the honoree joined the athletics director at midcourt, the crowd stood in unison and cheered wildly. Based on the decibel level, one would've thought Warlick had averaged 40 points per game. In fact, her four-year scoring average was a modest 6.4 points per game. Her career field-goal percentage was a so-so 43 percent, and her free throw percentage a nondescript 58 percent. Those numbers were more befitting a second-team role player than a first-team All-America player. So, why all the fuss?

The answer was obvious to anyone who had seen Frances Hollingsworth Warlick in action. She wasn't just a player, she was a phenomenon. She had enough charisma to fill a gymnasium and a bubbly grin that could illuminate it. She had a burst of speed that turned heads. She had a level of energy that defied description. And she had the kind of daring that kept her fans — and her coaches — on the edge of their seat.

True, she didn't score a lot of points. But she created hundreds with her flashy assists and prevented hundreds more with her amazing quickness, hustle, and instincts on defense. That's why Old Dominion's Nancy Lieberman, widely regarded as the greatest women's player of the era, respectfully dubbed her "the Secretary of Defense." And, just in case anyone doubted the distinction, Lieberman was more than willing to explain her reasoning.

"Everybody gains notoriety through points, but that's garbage," she said moments after the pesky Warlick limited her to 12 points in a 1980 game. "Somebody has to get the ball to you before you can score. On defense, it's just you. And Holly Warlick is the best."

Since Warlick and Lieberman had played with and against one another in numerous all-star competitions, one reporter suggested familiarity may have helped Warlick play Lieberman so tough defensively. Shaking her head emphatically, the Old Dominion star replied: "Holly could play [New York Knicks standout] Walt Frazier tough, and she's never even seen him."

Making Warlick's defensive prowess even more mind-boggling was the fact she never played defense prior to college. Tennessee high school girls of the 1970s could play offense or defense — but not *both* — due to the state's reluctance to abandon

Homegrown Holly Warlick came to Tennessee on a track scholarship but found fame in basketball.
UT Women's Media Relations

the archaic six-girl, half-court game. Because she possessed superior ballhandling and passing skills, Warlick played offense exclusively at Knoxville's Bearden High School.

Although she averaged better than 20 points per game as a three-year starter, Warlick achieved nothing beyond all-region honors on the high school hardwood. Conversely, she broke the state record in winning the 440-yard-dash title at the state track meet her senior year. And when she enrolled at the University of Tennessee a few months later, she did so on a track scholarship.

Since basketball was Warlick's second sport and defense was an unexplored frontier, Lady Vol coach Pat Head entertained some concerns regarding her ability to defend at the college level. To the coach's pleasant surprise, those concerns proved to be unfounded. By Warlick's senior season, Head noted: "I say without hesitation, she is the finest backcourt defensive player in America."

This ringing endorsement stemmed from a rare blend of physical and mental attributes—attributes that could be traced, at least in part, to Warlick's track background. Her dynamic style of play exhibited the burst of a sprinter, the endurance of a distance runner, and the leaping ability of a champion high jumper. Moreover, she showcased her fiercely competitive nature to fully exploit these remarkable physical gifts.

"There are a lot of talented athletes who lack desire," Head said. "And many athletes who aren't blessed with great talent compensate with determination. But Holly has both the innate abilities and the tremendous desire to take full advantage of them. It's that combination that makes her unique."

Warlick probably inherited some of her athleticism. Her father, Bill, played basketball at Duke University. Her mom, Fran, played basketball and field hockey at Winthrop College in

Rock Hill, North Carolina. An older brother played baseball at Cumberland (Kentucky) College. An older sister played recreation league basketball, prompting Holly—then a third-grader—to follow suit. "I decided to try out, too," she recalled. "I was a year too young for the league but they let me play anyway."

Following her prep career as a combination track/basketball star, Warlick sifted through several attractive scholarship offers. Ultimately, she chose Tennessee. For one thing, the campus was fifteen minutes from the family home. For another, she liked the fact Tennessee, with an enrollment of 30,000, was a major university. The school's rich sports tradition played a role in her decision, and so did the fact that Head had the women's basketball program on the rise. Since the women's track program was excellent as well, choosing Tennessee was a no-brainer.

Though signed to a track scholarship, Warlick admitted she had it "in the back of my mind that I wanted to put a lot of emphasis into basketball" once she enrolled on The Hill. Upon trying out for the hoops program, however, she found the adjustment from the six-player prep game to the five-player college game more difficult than she had anticipated. Two games into her Tennessee career, she was 2 of 13 from the field with just 2 assists.

"The problem has been adjusting to playing defense," she said in a comment that would prove humorously ironic later in life. "You're playing with two fewer people on the floor. It's a much faster game. In six-player ball, when the ball is at the other end of the floor, you can rest."

Anyone who ever saw Warlick play basketball assumed rest was a foreign concept to her. She seemed to be a perpetual-motion machine, capable of sustaining an incredible energy level for amazing stretches of time. If anything, she tended to play the game with too much abandon. "Coach tells me I'm not patient enough," she once explained. "I'm trying to develop patience. She also says I need to play under control—to be able to decide whether we can go through with the fastbreak."

Warlick almost single-handedly put the *fast* in the fastbreak at Tennessee. Even with her remarkable stamina, though, she found herself pushed to new levels of conditioning by Head. "She really works us hard," Warlick said two weeks into her college career. "It's no fun to outplay a team, then die near the end and lose. I don't think that will happen to us."

If meeting Head's expectations on the practice floor was tough, meeting the coach's expectations on the playing floor was even tougher. Warlick earned a starting job early in her freshman season but was yanked just 59 seconds into one game and benched for the remainder of the evening. "I wasn't playing too well," she noted sheepishly, "so I watched the rest of that one."

As she developed a better understanding of Head's system, Warlick's playing time and her effectiveness increased. She broke the single-game school record with 9 assists in her eighth college outing, an 82–57 romp at Kentucky. By Game 14, she had clearly established herself as the "stopper" on defense. Before a road game at Memphis State, Head presented the freshman point guard with a newspaper clipping extolling the virtues of Lady Tiger star Betty Booker. The coach then presented Warlick with a challenge: Stop her.

"That was the first time Pat ever came to me and said, 'You have to contain her for us to win,'" Warlick recalled. "We won, and I felt I contributed. That was my growing-up game. It made me realize what I had to do."

Warlick finished that freshman season with twenty-nine starts

Who's Superstitious?

One of the oldest clichés in sports suggests that luck occurs when preparation meets opportunity. Still, most athletes have some rituals they follow before every game . . . just in case.

Near the beginning of the 1977–78 season, Holly Warlick received a pair of 6-inch hugging monkey figures from her roommate, Suzanne Barbre. The stuffed animals, they agreed, were symbolic. "We took the monkeys with us everywhere," Warlick recalled. "They showed our closeness on the team."

When the Lady Vols won nine games in a row, the teammates came to view the monkeys as more than symbols; they had become good-luck charms. "Then we lost to Louisiana State; we pulled the monkeys apart," Warlick said. "When we won again, we put the monkeys back together again."

Tennessee carried a six-game winning streak into a February 11 game at the University of Alabama. Then the unthinkable happened. The roommates discovered mere hours before tipoff that they had left the monkeys back at their dormitory room. They hesitantly relayed this information to Tennessee's no-nonsense coach, Pat Head, then anxiously waited for her response.

"Pat went right out and found two monkeys just like mine," Warlick recalled. "Everybody got a big kick out of that."

Everybody except Alabama. The charmed Lady Vols went ape that night, pummeling the Tide 72–53.

in thirty-three games. She averaged just 3.8 points per game, shooting a mere 38.3 percent from the field and a paltry 48.9 percent from the foul line. She produced 112 assists, however, and enough defensive wizardry to help Tennessee place third in the Association of Intercollegiate Athletics for Women national tournament. There was no time to rest, however.

Once basketball season ended, Warlick joined the Lady Vol track team, competing in the 440-yard run and anchoring the mile relay unit. Shortly after helping Tennessee post a fourth-place finish in the AIAW Track and Field Nationals, she changed out of her track cleats and back into her basketball shoes. She earned two gold medals that summer while representing the United States in the Junior Pan-Am Games at Mexico City and the International Junior Tournament at Squaw Valley, California.

Undaunted by this brutally hectic pace, Warlick picked up where she left off as a Lady Vol sophomore in 1977–78. She tied her school record with 9 assists on January 17 against Middle Tennessee State, then shattered it with 14 assists on February 17 against Memphis State. She also recorded a couple of 7-steal games—December 12 against Ohio State and March 10 against Kentucky.

One of Warlick's finest performances unfolded December 17, 1977, in the Mississippi University for Women Christmas Tournament. She burned second-ranked Louisiana State for 13 points that evening and combined with backcourt mate Suzanne Barbre to force 27 turnovers as Tennessee notched a 72–63 upset. Warlick's tireless efforts at both ends of the floor even brought a smile to the face of her hard-to-please coach. "She'll battle," Head said. "She'll battle all day if she has to."

By season's end Warlick had nearly doubled her freshman scoring average, producing 6.6 points per game. She shot an exceptional 48.6 percent from the field, up 10 points from the year before. Her free throw percentage—though less than inspiring at 53.1—was up 4 points from the previous season.

Street and Smith's magazine was impressed enough to accord her second-team All-America recognition.

After nineteen months of almost nonstop competition in two sports, even the energetic Warlick was exhausted. Grudgingly, she decided to give up track and concentrate on basketball. That was a wise move. She put together several outstanding games as a junior in 1978–79, but probably her best occurred January 5 against defending national champ UCLA. Doing a little bit of everything, she contributed 8 points, 7 assists, 6 rebounds, and 6 steals in an 88–74 victory. Three weeks later, she recorded a 9-assist game against Louisiana State. "I would rather make a good pass than score myself," she explained.

Even so, her junior scoring average held steady at 6.4 points per game. Her field-goal percentage (43.8) slipped a bit from the year before, but her free throw percentage (69.0) jumped 15 points from the previous season. Moreover, she registered 141 steals, setting a single-season program record that still stands a quarter-century later. After leading Tennessee to another Final Four, she again was named All-American.

Warlick's wizardry as a ballhandler/defensive ace soared to new heights during her final go-round as a Lady Vol in 1979–80. She recorded 12 assists against Clemson on March 5, 1980, and registered 10 on four other occasions—versus Vanderbilt on November 12, 1979; versus North Carolina State on New Year's Day of 1980; versus Memphis State on January 21, 1980; and versus Ole Miss on February 10, 1980. Her finest defensive games—statistically, at least—were 8-steal efforts against UCLA on December 19, 1979, and against Louisiana State on January 20, 1980.

In addition to averaging a career-high 6.9 points per game as a senior, she shattered her own school record for assists. Tabbed

Praise from on High

The selection committee for the Kodak All-America team had to be impressed by a letter it received in early February of 1979. It read:

> I would like to recommend Holly Warlick for the 1979 Kodak All-American team. Holly, as I see her, is the spark of the Tennessee team. She moves fast, quarterbacks beautifully for the team and is a pleasure to watch, even though she is not on our team. She cuts the passing lanes to perfection and I think it couldn't be better said than what our own Debbie Brock, Kodak All-American, 1978, said several times: "We would have a better chance with Tennessee if Holly Warlick would foul out on the first play of the game." She just happened to be playing opposite her each time.
>
> Sincerely,
>
> Margaret Wade, Head Coach
> Lady Statesmen, D.S.U.

Yes, the letter was penned by that Margaret Wade, the legendary Delta State University coach for whom the prestigious Wade Trophy was named.

All-American for the third year in a row, Warlick left behind a remarkable legacy. Her four years had produced a 118–23 record, a Southeastern Conference Tournament title, and three Final Four bids. "I was lucky," she modestly explained, "because it seems like I came here just as the program really started to grow."

Warlick's enthusiasm is still evident today in her role as Lady Vol assistant.
Randy Moore/Rocky Top News

Of course, Warlick played a major role in that growth. "She's been a great inspiration to her teammates," Head said. "Holly wouldn't settle for just being good. She was determined to become better than that. She's one of the finest athletes I've ever seen, and I've seen plenty."

Perhaps the greatest testament to Warlick's skills as a player is this: Twenty-five years after she concluded her illustrious career, she still ranks first on the school's all-time list in single-season steals (141), second in single-season assists (225), second in single-game assists (14), second in career assists (673), and third in single-game steals (9).

Despite her consummate skills as a passer, ballhandler, and defender, Warlick is best remembered for her boundless enthusiasm and dogged determination. She played each game as if it were her last, routinely finishing with sweat covering her face and floor burns covering her legs. "I don't mind a few scabs on my knees," she quipped, "because I don't have the prettiest legs around anyway. I doubt I'd win a beauty contest with 'em."

Probably not. Had Frances Hollingsworth Warlick entered a beauty pageant in those days, however, she most assuredly would've claimed the "Miss Congeniality" award. There has never been a more popular player in Lady Vol basketball, and there probably never will be.

Good as Gold

In the beginning—before bling-bling had a name—there was Gordon. Prior to each Lady Vol basketball game played between the fall of 1985 and the spring of 1989, Bridgette Gordon removed fifteen gold chains from her neck. She removed fourteen gold rings from her fingers—nine from the left hand, five from the right. She removed four gold earrings from her left ear, five from the right. She removed four gold bracelets from her left wrist, five from the right. She removed a gold bracelet from her right ankle and a gold watch from her left wrist. Somehow, she got all of this accomplished by tipoff.

"I love gold," she would say. "It's just me. It's what I'm into."

Capping the show, literally, was a gold-trimmed tooth with a gold inlaid "B" on it. Fortunately, she didn't have to remove it before taking the floor. "I thought about going all gold with the tooth," she once explained, "but Coach Summitt isn't too big on all this stuff in the first place, and I thought I better not push my luck."

Resembling Fort Knox in sneakers, Gordon made quite an impression during her early days at Tennessee. It wasn't always a favorable impression, though. She looked like a prima donna, and she sometimes behaved like a prima donna. This posed an obvious problem, since Summitt despises prima donnas—even talented ones.

Certainly, there was no mistaking Gordon's talent. Her career averages at DeLand (Florida) High School included 31 points and 15 rebounds per game. As a junior, she led her team to the state title. As a senior, she was closing in on the state record for points. Her bid would end abruptly, however, when she was ruled ineligible after flunking both Spanish and math. Gordon's ineligibility was a great disappointment to her teammates, but it wasn't the first time Gordon had let someone down, and it wouldn't be the last time.

Summitt—the strict, demanding, and uncompromising perfectionist—traveled to DeLand in 1985 to meet with Gordon—the immature, undisciplined, and ineligible symbol of imperfection. What the coach saw was a player who exhibited everything a typical Tennessee recruit was not. She also saw a player whose remarkable skills could help Tennessee claim that elusive first national title. After six unsuccessful trips to the Final Four, Summitt was willing

More Surly than Girlie

In social settings Bridgette Gordon was the picture of femininity during her Lady Vol basketball days. Her attire was always fashionable. Her hair was always neat and stylish. Her jewelry was always eye-catching, and her manners were always impeccable. She was all woman—off the court.

On the court, however, she was all beast. She'd throw elbows at her opponents. She'd talk smack, then back it up. She'd scowl at officials who dared to whistle her for a foul. She'd fight for rebounds the way a hungry lion fights for the final scraps of a fresh kill. "I guess I'm just an animal when I'm on the court," she explained. "Sometimes I don't even realize what I'm doing."

Obviously. Whistled for an offensive foul in the first half of a 1988 game against the University of Washington, Gordon shot an icy glare at the official, then underscored her contempt by rolling the ball out of bounds. As the official chased after the ball, Lady Vol coach Pat Summitt summoned Gordon to the bench, where the senior captain spent the remainder of the first half and the opening moments of the second. It was the first time since her freshman year Gordon had failed to start a second half.

Afterward, she admitted her treatment of the official was inappropriate . . . well, sort of. "A couple of years ago I probably would have said something I shouldn't have and threw the ball at him," she said. "I'm getting better at that . . ."

to gamble on this talented but temperamental superstar. The coach offered a scholarship, and Gordon accepted. Theirs would be a match made in hell—or at least purgatory.

One week later, the University of Florida offered Gordon a scholarship, and she accepted that one, too. Early the next morning Summitt awoke to the phone ringing. A coaching friend had called to share the not-so-pleasant news. "No!" Summitt shouted into the mouthpiece.

Yes, the report was true. What's more, Gordon had committed to several other schools before committing to Tennessee and Florida. The Sunshine State superstar, it seemed, was just a girl who couldn't say no—at least not to college recruiters. An angry Summitt considered the distinct possibility that Gordon was a player who carried even more baggage than talent and would be a poor fit for Tennessee. "I can't stay in this," the coach thought. "It's not worth it."

As time passed, Summitt regained her composure—relatively speaking, at least—and telephoned the Gordon residence. The fact Bridgette was unavailable may have been fortunate, because coach and player alike might have regretted the exchange that probably would've taken place in that tension-filled moment. When Summitt and Gordon finally hooked up by phone later that day, the coach delivered a polite but firm ultimatum: "You give me a solid commitment or I give your scholarship to someone else."

Gordon gave her word. Of course, her word was about as valuable as a two-dollar watch . . . and considerably less reliable. "I probably committed to everybody who talked to me," Gordon recalled years later. "At that point in time, I felt like it was a crime to say no, so I always said yes." She couldn't even say no to offi-

A Familiar Story Line

Bridgette Gordon's parents divorced when she was very young. Because her mother worked two jobs and had seven other children, Bridgette essentially was reared by a devoted and deeply religious grandmother, Frances Phillips.

Tall for her age, Bridgette began playing playground basketball against boys. Realizing she could compete on even terms with them convinced her she might have a future on the hardwood. Heavily recruited following a standout high school career, she chose the University of Tennessee.

Bridgette's college achievements included four Final Fours and two national titles. Twice she was named All-American. She graduated as the leading scorer—male or female—in school history.

Now flash forward ten years and consider the life of Chamique Holdsclaw:

Her parents divorced when she was very young. Because her mother was struggling financially, Chamique essentially was reared by a devoted and deeply religious grandmother, June Holdsclaw.

Tall for her age, Chamique began playing playground basketball against boys. Realizing she could compete on even terms with them convinced her she might have a future on the hardwood. Heavily recruited following a standout high school career, she chose the University of Tennessee.

Chamique's college achievements included four Final Fours and three national titles. Four times she was named All-American. She graduated as the leading scorer—male or female—in school history.

Sound familiar?

cial visits—agreeing to several she never intended to make, then leaving school officials waiting anxiously at their local airports to greet a player who would never arrive.

Because Tennessee was a high-profile program located reasonably close to home, Gordon went against her nature and actually honored her Lady Vol commitment. Of course, commitment was a somewhat vague concept for her at the time. In Gordon's vocabulary, commitment meant showing up for practice—usually on time. "I guess I had more talent than a lot of other people," she recalled. "And, instead of working hard, I would just coast."

Anyone who has attended a Pat Summitt practice—or even heard about a Pat Summitt practice—knows the ultra-intense Lady Vol coach does not tolerate players who "just coast." Thus, the early days of preseason practice in October 1985 were not pleasant ones. The more Summitt snapped and snarled, the more Gordon responded with a sneer or a roll of the eyes. "I was a butt," she later said, choosing the most flattering euphemism available.

Being strong-willed and a bit arrogant, Gordon could not admit *she* was the problem. It had to be Summitt, the sharp-tongued woman with the impossible standards and the ice-melting glare. Gordon figured all of her problems would be solved if she could merely escape the clutches of this evil taskmaster. So she tried. And tried. And tried.

Dozens of times Bridgette called home. Dozens of times her mom, Marjorie, told her to sit tight, that things would get better. And they did . . . eventually. One day, an exasperated Summitt took her petulant young superstar aside and uttered the magic words that finally put everything in perspective: "No one can stop you."

Thereafter, no one *did*. Gordon quit whining and began shining. She won a starting job in preseason and posted a double-

double (17 points, 12 rebounds) in her second varsity game, a 71–57 defeat of Illinois.

Still, old habits die hard, and Gordon's laid-back attitude in a 74–53 Game 3 loss to Texas bumped her from the starting lineup for Tennessee's next nine games. Having learned her lesson, she came off the bench in Games 4 and 5 to score 20 points against Kansas State and 16 against Eastern Illinois. Three consecutive single-digit scoring efforts followed, but Gordon got back on track in Games 9 through 13 against Toledo (19 points), Hawaii Pacific (21), West Virginia (10), South Carolina (18), and East Tennessee State (15).

Returned to the starting lineup for Game 13 against North Carolina, Gordon was so unnerved she hit just 2 of 14 field-goal tries and committed 6 turnovers. She atoned by grabbing 10 rebounds, however, including 5 off the offensive backboard. Rewarded with another start in Game 14, she responded with a 24-point, 7-rebound, 4-steal effort against North Carolina State.

A few uneven performances later, she was benched for Game 20 against Georgia. Clearly motivated by the move, she came off the bench to produce 20 points and 17 rebounds in a sizzling twenty-nine-minute relief stint. Incredibly, Gordon would hit double-figures in fifteen of Tennessee's final sixteen games. Even more incredible was the poise she showed while registering a 17-point, 10-rebound effort in a NCAA Final Four semifinal loss to Cheryl Miller and Southern Cal.

That 1985–86 season saw Gordon notch two notable achievements. She was the first Lady Vol ever voted Southeastern Conference Freshman of the Year and the first freshman ever to lead Tennessee in scoring (14.2 points per game). Still, the best was yet to come.

Gordon's offensive exploits had been so impressive no one seemed to notice the progress she made defensively in the final weeks of her debut season. They noticed in the opening weeks of the 1986–87 season, however. When Tennessee shocked top-ranked Texas 85–78 on December 14 in Austin, ending the defending national champ Longhorns' forty-game home winning streak, Gordon did the expected: pacing the offense with 26 points. But she also did the unexpected: limiting All-America Andrea Lloyd to 3 shots and 2 points while frustrating her into 9 turnovers.

"Bridgette did a tremendous job on Andrea Lloyd," Summitt said. Gordon's sheepish response? "In high school, playing defense was nonexistent to me."

With Gordon contributing at both ends of the floor, the Lady Vols swept through the regular season with a 22–5 record. One of the losses was a 75–69 setback at Auburn. Auburn beat Tennessee again in the semifinals of the Southeastern Conference tournament. This time Joe Ciampi's high-octane Lady Tigers prevailed 102–96.

With Gordon stuck in a two-week slump, Tennessee's chances of returning to the Final Four appeared slim. She showed signs of breaking loose in the Lady Vols' first-round NCAA Tournament game—scoring 23 points in a 95–59 blowout of Tennessee Tech—but her struggles resumed in the Mideast Region semifinals against Virginia. She managed just 4 points in those first twenty minutes, and Tennessee managed a scant 26–24 lead. Had she been small enough to fit inside her locker, Gordon surely would've hidden there during the intermission. Instead, she settled for standing near the dressing room door. "I was trying to sneak out," she recalled. "I knew she [Summitt] was going to try to talk to me at the half."

Bridgette Gordon proved too quick for taller players and too strong for smaller players.
UT Women's Media Relations

Sure enough, the Lady Vol coach sought out her star player, then offered a few words of wisdom: "Settle down. You need to be relaxed."

The advice worked. Gordon scored 17 second-half points, including 15 in the game's final 10:57, as Tennessee rallied to win 66–58. Her line score was an impressive one: 9 of 13 from the field, 3 of 3 from the foul line, and 21 points in just twenty-five minutes.

Never one to mince words, Summitt cut to the chase when addressing the media at game's end. "Bridgette's been hiding the last two weeks," the coach said. "I thought she responded well with the big plays."

The way Gordon saw it, her offense returned when her focus on offense returned. "During that two-week period in my slump, I was concentrating on my defense, and I think that's when I lost my rhythm," she said. "The coaches told me if I could get that back, the Bridgette Gordon of the beginning of the season would come back. I'm shooting with a lot of confidence, like I did at the beginning."

That was fortunate, because Tennessee's next game would be the Mideast finals against Auburn. In addition to a pair of victories over Tennessee, the Lady Tigers had been mauling everyone else in women's basketball, as evidenced by their 31–1 record and number two national ranking. Determined to redeem herself following a subpar performance in the loss to Auburn just fifteen days earlier, Gordon was all business as she took the floor for pregame warm-ups. This time, she vowed, would be different.

It was. Playing as if her very soul were at stake, she took control in the opening minutes and dominated the game from start to finish. She concluded the evening with 33 points, 10 rebounds, and just one turnover in thirty-eight minutes of inspired play as the Lady Vols trounced the Lady Tigers 77–61.

Afterward, accepting the regional tourney's Most Valuable Player award was a mere formality.

"I remembered how I felt when Auburn beat us in Albany at the SEC Tournament," Gordon said. "Tonight, I just had one thing in mind: Auburn wasn't going to beat us on our home court."

As things turned out, no one would beat Tennessee on *any* court the rest of the season. The Lady Vols rolled into Austin, Texas, with high hopes and rolled out four days later with their first-ever national championship. Gordon led the charge by producing two double-doubles—21 points and 11 rebounds in a 74–64 defeat of Long Beach State, then 13 points and 12 rebounds in a smashing 67–44 defeat of Louisiana Tech in the title game.

Bridgette Gordon had guided Tennessee to the top of women's basketball. And she was only a sophomore.

Gordon's junior season began the way her sophomore season ended—in fairy-tale fashion. Playing barely twenty-five minutes per game, she led the Lady Vols to lopsided defeats of Indiana (91–52), Old Dominion (83–52), and Stetson (102–59). The fairy tale ended abruptly, however, when she was limited to 10 points on 3–of–14 shooting in a humbling 97–79 home-floor loss to Texas.

Tennessee bounced back to win six games in a row. But when Gordon endured another off night (8 points on 4–of–12 shooting), Tennessee endured another home-floor loss, bowing 71–68 to Auburn. Suddenly, the defending national champs appeared vulnerable. With the Lady Vols desperately needing guidance, Gordon provided it. No longer the self-centered "butt" she had been earlier, she took her game to a previously unimagined level over the next two months. She led. Teammates followed. Opponents wilted.

Informed by assistant coach Holly Warlick that she wasn't using her legs enough in her shooting stroke, Gordon took the tip to heart. She registered 30 points in a 91–68 drubbing of Old Dominion, then followed with 26 in a 104–67 dismantling of Vanderbilt. A 25-point effort in an 85–80 road win at South Carolina preceded a 22-point performance in a 97–70 thrashing of Alabama. Gordon scored 28 points in twenty-eight minutes as Tennessee routed Memphis 97–73, added 20 in an 82–79 squeaker at Georgia, then contributed 26 more in a 91–71 romp at Notre Dame.

Her string of 20-point games ended at Game 7 with a 17-point showing in a 78–67 win at Ole Miss, so Gordon started a new string. She scored 24 in an 81–74 defeat of Mississippi State, 28 in an 89–82 defeat of Louisiana State, 23 in a 76–74 victory over number five Louisiana Tech, and 21 in a 99–75 trouncing of Kentucky.

In the defeat of Louisiana State, Gordon produced 24 second-half points, prompting Lady Tiger coach Sue Gunter to note: "When Gordon's playing like that, quite frankly, I don't think anybody in the country could stop her." Meanwhile, Summitt's praise of Gordon was tempered with a bit of sarcasm: "We've got to convince her that if she can play that well the whole game, she could average 40 points a game."

In the Tech game, Gordon produced 17 second-half points as the Lady Vols rallied from a 41–32 intermission deficit. "I had to come out and be Superwoman," she said, adding that Summitt "told me to go out and prove I could play against anyone."

The Lady Vol standout certainly proved that point to Lady Techster coach Leon Barmore, who rhetorically asked: "How do you stop a great player like Gordon?"

Two weeks later, Gordon headed for the Southeastern Conference Tournament with her confidence soaring. She scored 20 points in just twenty minutes as Tennessee pounded Kentucky 100–66; then she hit 32 in an 82–76 defeat of Georgia that left Lady Bulldog coach Andy Landers shaking his head in awe. "I thought our one problem was Bridgette Gordon," he said. "She did an incredible job coming to the front for Tennessee. And I thought Tennessee did an excellent job recognizing that she wanted to play."

Apparently, Gordon "wanted to play" again the next night. She nailed 13 of 18 field-goal tries and scored 34 points as Tennessee nipped Auburn 73–70 in the finals. Gushed teammate Sheila Frost: "When things are going her way, she can do anything. She was just moving constantly, and no one could stop her."

Gordon conceded the point, matter-of-factly noting: "No one was stopping me, so I took the shots." She took enough shots in the three league tournament games to be tabbed Most Valuable Player. Her numbers told the story: She averaged 28.7 points per game, while shooting 58 percent from the floor and 80 percent from the foul line.

Gordon continued her torrid play in the NCAA Tournament, recording 20 of her 28 points in the second half as Tennessee routed Wake Forest 94–66 in Round 1. After a 13-point effort against James Madison in the East Region semifinals, she scored 20 points in the region finals against Virginia, helping the Lady Vols reach their third consecutive Final Four. Advancing to Tacoma, however, Tennessee ran into a red-hot Louisiana Tech team. Gordon hit 7 of 13 shots but the Lady Vols fell 68–59 in the semifinal round.

After guiding Tennessee to three Final Fours in three years, Gordon's legacy was secure. "Bridgette has put basketball on the map at Tennessee," Summitt said. "We were good when Bridgette came here, but she put us on the national map."

Who's That Guy Talking to Bridgette?

Shortly after winning her second NCAA Tournament championship in 1989, Bridgette Gordon joined the rest of Tennessee's players and coaches for the traditional White House visit to accept congratulations from the president of the United States.

Understandably, several of the Lady Vols were a little nervous about meeting George Bush. Not Gordon. Having met the president following Tennessee's first-ever NCAA title two years earlier, she considered the leader of the free world to be a bosom buddy. So, when President Bush offered a handshake and a smile, Gordon reciprocated by offering something of her own: an autographed photo of herself.

The president was speechless.

Surrounded by a great supporting cast, Gordon carried less of the scoring load during her senior year in 1988–89. Still, she enjoyed some memorable moments. Sixteen points in Game 3 against Louisiana Tech made her the leading scorer in Lady Vol history. With 10 against Southern Illinois she hit the 2,000-point mark. With 34 in the regular-season finale against Alabama, she passed former Volunteer Ernie Grunfeld to become the leading scorer—male or female—in university history. Her highlights also included a 24-point, 8-assist effort against Stanford, 24 points against Rutgers, 25 against Vanderbilt, 29 against Louisiana Tech, and 30 against Western Kentucky.

Gordon's greatest thrill of the regular season, however, occurred in her hometown. Summitt had scheduled a game in DeLand against Stetson, and a capacity crowd of 3,760 turned out to watch its hometown heroine in action. Gordon didn't disappoint, scoring 23 points as the Lady Vols romped 97–62. "It was a great feeling, being home with all this support," she said afterward. "I never had this many fans in high school."

Saving her best for last, Gordon caught fire in postseason play. She scored 25 points against Auburn in the Southeastern Conference title game and 29 against LaSalle in first-round NCAA Tournament play. She followed with 21 points against Virginia and 33 against Long Beach State in the East Regional, earning Tennessee a fourth consecutive bid to the Final Four. There, in a fitting farewell to college basketball, Gordon scored 27 points—tying the championship game record—to guide the Lady Vols past Auburn 76–60 for their second national title in three years.

No one was happier to see Gordon exhaust her collegiate eligibility than Auburn coach Joe Ciampi. "God bless her, graduate and get out of Tennessee," he said. "It seems like we played her for a lifetime."

The NCAA Tournament wasn't the only title Gordon won during her final season of amateur basketball competition. Despite a dislocated finger, she made the U.S. Olympic team that competed at the 1988 Games in Seoul, South Korea. Though cast in the role of defensive stopper, she scored 20 points in a win over Yugoslavia and averaged 8.8 points per game in helping the United States capture the championship. Later, at the awards ceremony, she stood on the podium with a big smile on her face and a gaudy medal draped around her neck.

Gold, of course.

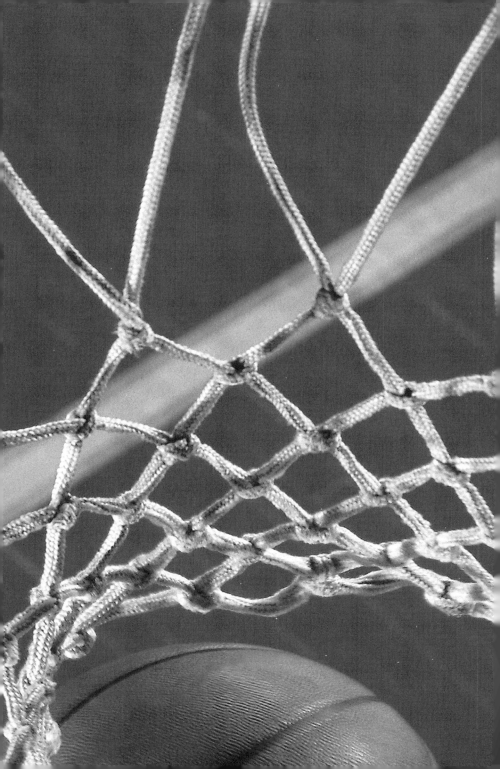

The Corn-fed Chicks

When a team making its first Final Four appearance draws a team making its eighth appearance, the former should be nervous and the latter should be loose. But that wasn't the case when Long Beach State's 49ers and Tennessee's Lady Vols prepared to square off at Austin, Texas, in March of 1987.

The upstart 49ers didn't show any jitters. Heck, they didn't even show any respect.

"We've played Tennessee and beaten them twice [1979 and 1983] since I've been coaching here," head coach Joan Bonvicini said on the eve of the NCAA semifinals. "We're confident. If we were from the Southeast, maybe Tennessee's reputation would have an effect."

Those were bold words—arrogant words, perhaps—but the Long Beach players were even cockier than their coach. Point guard Penny Toler was downright boastful as she discussed the 49ers' nearly unstoppable transition attack. "When it's three-on-three, we don't wait for the other two players; we'll be looking to score," she said. "When it's three-on-four, we still might be."

Toler's confidence was well-founded. Long Beach boasted the most explosive offense in the history of women's collegiate basketball. The 49ers averaged 94.4 points per game with an imposing 32.5-point victory margin. They had obliterated the NCAA's single-season records for points (3,304), field goals (1,386), and 100-point games (15), peaking with a 149–69 annihilation of San Jose State. Two-time All-American Cindy Brown had scored an NCAA-record 60 points that night.

Moreover, Long Beach was coming off an eye-popping performance in the West Regional. The 49ers had crushed Ole Miss 84–55 in the semifinals and trounced Ohio State 102–82 in the title game behind 40 points from Brown. The California team had a better record (33–2) than Tennessee (26–6) and a higher ranking (number four) than Tennessee (number seven). The 49ers also owned a victory over Louisiana Tech, a team that had dumped the Lady Vols by 12 points just six weeks earlier. Throw in the fact Tennessee had been to seven previous Final Fours without winning one, and Long Beach found no reason to be intimidated.

"Not at all," Bonvicini said, rubbing a little more salt into the wound.

While Long Beach was showing no respect for Tennessee, Lady Vol head coach Pat Summitt was showing plenty of respect for the 49ers. "I'm convinced they're the quickest team in America," she said. "We can run *at* them at times, but we can't go in with the idea that we're going to run *with* them."

Summitt even acknowledged Long Beach's apparent superiority. "I know that someone's going to want to know how I feel about going to seven Final Fours and never winning one," she said. "To tell the truth, we haven't had the personnel to win in most of them. We've never been favored to win it, and we'll be underdogs again this time. That's all right with me. This team likes to play as the underdog."

Given Tennessee's knack for Final Four futility and Long Beach's knack for piling up points, their March 27 showdown projected to be another smashing victory for the 49ers and another disappointment for the Lady Vols. But projections don't always come true.

Toler discovered as much the first time she dribbled across midcourt in the game's opening minute. As she signaled the offensive set to her teammates, Tennessee's players responded by calling out what play was coming. The 49ers attacked the basket aggressively, but the Lady Vols repelled the attack even more aggressively. And so it went, possession after possession.

"We had worked so hard on Long Beach's plays this week in practice we knew them better than they did," Tennessee's Bridgette Gordon said. "Us calling out their plays really frustrated them. Toler didn't know what to do."

Nor did Brown. Long Beach's 6'2" superstar was continuously bumped, jostled, and frustrated by a rotation of burly Tennessee post players that included 6'4" Sheila Frost, 6'2" Kathy Spinks, and 6'2" Karla Horton.

Kathy Spinks was a key player in Tennessee's 1987 title run.
UT Women's Media Relations

As a result, with 4:30 left in the game, the Lady Vols and 49ers were deadlocked at 55–55. Then, as so often happens in marquee matchups, an obscure player stole the spotlight. Melissa McCray, who shot just 43 percent from the field during the regular season, nailed a long jump shot for Tennessee. Then she hit another. Gordon scored inside, Dawn Marsh added 2 free throws, and Gordon added another to complete a 9–0 run that gave the Lady Vols a 64–55 lead with 2:21 remaining. With freshman Tonya Edwards hitting 6 of 6 free throws down the stretch, Tennessee prevailed 74–64, limiting Long Beach to its lowest point total of the season.

"That number 35 [McCray] surprised us from the outside," Bonvicini noted. "Nothing in our scouting report had prepared us for that. She was hitting three-pointers out there."

The three-point basket already was in effect for men's play, but the women's game had not yet adopted it. Still, McCray's timely two-pointers—she finished 5 of 7 from the floor—turned the tide in Tennessee's favor and thrilled her teammates on the Lady Vol bench. "They were saying, 'Shoot, Melissa, shoot!' because Long Beach wasn't playing me," McCray said. "I wasn't even thinking about it. I just did what I would do in practice."

McCray's bubbly enthusiasm provided a stark contrast to Brown's brooding postgame demeanor. Although the 49ers' star matched her regular-season scoring average with 27 points and pulled down a Final Four semifinal record 18 rebounds, she was less than gracious in defeat. "There were some cheap shots out there," the slender standout grumbled. "It wasn't basketball. But what do you expect from big corn-fed chicks like that?"

One of the "corn-fed chicks" who had guarded Brown laughed when told of the comment. "She should talk," Horton said. "She almost broke my ribs with an elbow."

The Lady Vols' postgame elation was short-lived. They showered and dressed just in time to watch Louisiana Tech close out a 79–75 upset of Texas to earn the other berth in Sunday's title game. Tennessee's record against Tech was a pitiful 1–11. Worse, the Lady Techsters had won the past ten meetings in the series, including a 72–60 verdict just six weeks earlier.

Acutely aware of all this, Summitt, along with aides Mickie DeMoss and Holly Warlick, sat up watching film of Louisiana Tech until 3:00 A.M. Upon finishing the task, Summitt felt both fatigued and relieved. "For the first time," she said, "I began to think that I knew what the Louisiana Tech offense was all about."

With the NCAA title game scheduled for Sunday, March 29, Saturday was set aside for preparation, news conferences, and reflection. Summitt found her thoughts wandering to a trip to Austin three months earlier. On December 14 her team had stunned top-ranked Texas 85–78, ending the defending national champs' forty-game winning streak. The Lady Longhorns led 78–76 with 3:01 to play, but Tennessee had scored the game's final 9 points.

"It certainly looked different to see a team taking it to us, and us being the tentative ones," Texas coach Jody Conradt said. Meanwhile, Summitt called the performance "a great team effort," adding, "Today's game rates in my top ten, maybe five or six."

Two weeks later, however, Texas avenged the setback. Shooting 54 percent from the field, the Lady Longhorns trounced Tennessee 88–74 in the Orange Bowl Invitational at Coral Gables, Florida. "I'm just really searching for what we need to do with our postgame," Summitt said. "I've been searching since [practice began on] October 15th."

The Lady Vols gave their coach her 300th victory on January 4, forcing 34 turnovers in an 87–68 defeat of North Carolina. One month later, however, Tennessee was thoroughly outclassed by homestanding Louisiana Tech. "As poorly as we played, we're probably fortunate to be leaving Ruston only 12 down," Summitt grumbled. "The bottom line is, they're very well coached. They play a smart game, and they're mentally tough."

Tennessee's mental toughness, meanwhile, was a bit suspect. After finishing the regular season 22–5, the Lady Vols were looking for some momentum when they pulled into Albany, Georgia, for the Southeastern Conference Tournament. They didn't find it. After edging Louisiana State 64–63 in their tourney opener, they bowed to Auburn 102–96 in the semifinals. Tennessee's two-game stats showed Horton making just 5 of 19 field-goal tries, Gordon 8 of 24, Frost 3 of 8, and senior captain Shelley Sexton 2 of 10. It was no exaggeration to say the Lady Vols would be limping into the NCAA Tournament.

Still, Tennessee's players were talking a good game, even though it had been a while since they'd played a good one. "We're not dwelling on what happened at the SEC Tournament," Horton said. "I don't know what happened down there except that we just didn't play well."

Facing Tennessee Tech in round one of the NCAA Tournament, Summitt decided to bench her top three scorers: Gordon (15.5 points per game), Frost (11.5), and Horton (10.0). Horton accepted the demotion philosophically, noting: "I think we've learned that no matter who starts, we've got to go out there ready to play because what happens early affects the whole game."

What happened early in this game was a Tennessee blitz. The Lady Vols led 15–2 after six minutes and 25–6 after nine. It

From Chumps to Champs

Although Tennessee's players were a heartbroken bunch after suffering a 102–96 setback to Auburn in the 1987 Southeastern Conference Tournament, the defeat proved to be a blessing. They lost the game but regained their focus. Three weeks later, the team that wasn't good enough to win the league championship proved good enough to win the national championship.

"The SEC Tournament was the key; it opened our eyes," head coach Pat Summitt noted. "This team played as hard in the NCAA as any team I've ever been around."

Senior captain Shelley Sexton also pinpointed the Auburn loss as the season's turning point. "Sometimes you have to go through hard times to get to where you want to go," she said. "We could either fight or give up, and we weren't about to give up."

Recognizing that her squad lacked the overall quickness and athleticism to keep pace with teams of Auburn's skill level, Summitt essentially reinvented her team. Instead of playing run-and-gun on offense and full-court pressure on defense, the Lady Vols became a more deliberate and efficient team at both ends of the floor. The coach also benched three of her starters.

"I think putting people in their place was the difference," Summitt said shortly after trouncing Louisiana Tech 67–44 in the NCAA title game. "Everybody began playing their role. They all put the 'I' out of it except from the perspective of how 'I' can help the team. We did not have a good chemistry until the national tournament started. That's when they started listening. They became a lot more coachable. They became more determined."

Ultimately, they became champions.

was 47–20 at halftime and 95–59 at the finish. Gordon came off the bench to score 23 points in twenty-eight minutes. "It was a test, a challenge for me," she said. "It's not important for me to start; it's important for Tennessee to win."

It would take more than a home-floor defeat of tiny Tennessee Tech to convince Summitt her team was back on the right track, however. "Playing on your own floor," she mused, "is like driving your own car."

As fate would have it, the Lady Vols would continue playing on their own floor. They were to host the Mideast Regional, which also featured Virginia, Old Dominion, and Auburn. Tennessee and Virginia were paired in one semifinal game, with Old Dominion and Auburn colliding in the other.

"Our lineup is up for grabs," Summitt said. "We're playing better now than we played in Albany. We have to play well to beat Virginia. We're not as good a basketball team as Virginia, ODU, or Auburn."

That assessment appeared prophetic when, with twelve minutes remaining, the Lady Vols trailed Virginia 39–33. Disgusted with her team's defensive effort, Summitt called timeout and switched from man-to-man to a 1–3–1 zone. Tennessee quickly went on a 12–2 run that produced a 45–41 lead and, eventually, a 66–58 victory.

Cavalier coach Debbie Ryan saluted Summitt, noting: "Unfortunately, the timeout Pat called was perfect. That was the turning point of the game."

Summitt's next challenge was to find a way to win the region final against an Auburn team that already had beaten Tennessee during the regular season (76–69) and the league tournament (102–96). The Lady Vols' start was hardly auspicious. They went five minutes without scoring, allowing the Lady Tigers to grab a 13–6 lead.

Auburn led 37–34 early in the second half, but Tennessee's defensive pressure finally began to wear down the Lady Tigers. As a result, the Lady Vols outscored the visitors 43–24 the rest of the way and romped 77–61. All-American Vicki Orr, who torched Tennessee in the two earlier meetings, managed just 13 points this time. "Tonight," Summitt said, "we played tremendous defense with tremendous intensity."

Losing coach Joe Ciampi agreed, graciously declining to blame the defeat on Tennessee's home-court advantage. "Nobody went out there and helped them play defense," he said. "The way they played tonight, they could have probably done it any place. They could have probably gone on top of the Holiday Inn and done a job."

Gordon, returned to the starting lineup, responded with 33 points and 10 rebounds en route to recognition as the regional tourney's most valuable player. "It really doesn't matter if I start," she said. "They were getting me the ball when I was hot. You're seeing a different Bridgette Gordon."

Fans were seeing a different Tennessee, too. As Gordon noted: "If we play the way we played tonight, we'll bring home a national championship."

Now, with the Lady Vols mere hours from playing for that championship, Summitt smiled at the recollection. Gordon had the talent to back up her boast, but she would need help from the "corn-fed chicks"—Frost, Horton, and Spinks—if Tennessee was to upend Louisiana Tech in the title game.

Frost, from the tiny midstate town of Pulaski, had come to Tennessee with one half-decent post move DeMoss jokingly called "the Pulaski Shuffle." She had made tremendous strides in her first two years on campus, however, and now ranked with the top centers in women's basketball.

The Wit and Wisdom of Sheila Frost

The first thing people always noticed about Tennessee's Sheila Frost was her remarkable size. At 6'4", she towered above most folks. The second thing people noticed was her remarkable candor. Once, after being thoroughly outplayed by Auburn All-American Vicki Orr, Frost mused: "My uniform was there, my body was there, but I wasn't there."

When head coach Pat Summitt benched her following a subpar effort in the 1987 Southeastern Conference Tournament at Albany, Georgia, Frost admitted her calm exterior sometimes masked a raging storm. "I didn't get mad at Pat for benching me," she said. "I got so excited during warm-ups that I couldn't get anything done for a while. Sitting on the bench for a few minutes gave me time to get settled down."

Looking back on Tennessee's lopsided loss to Southern Cal in the 1986 Final Four, Frost noted: "Last year our goal was just to get to the Final Four. We made it, we got blown out, and that was it."

When asked about facing a Long Beach State team making its first Final Four appearance, Frost was even more brutally frank: "We know what it's like to choke. This year the team we're playing hasn't been to the Final Four, so they could come in hyper and fold, just like we did last year."

Not surprisingly, when Tennessee rallied from its disappointing performance in the 1987 conference tourney to win the NCAA Tournament three weeks later, it was Frost who did the best job of putting the achievement in proper perspective: "We knew all along that we were number one, but this proves it," she said, pausing before sheepishly adding: "We wondered about it a little bit down in Albany, though."

Sheila Frost showcased some nice moves and a refreshing candor.
UT Women's Media Relations

"Sheila has all the tools, all the potential in the world," Summitt had said two weeks earlier. "She can be pretty much what she decides she wants to be."

Frost conceded the point, noting: "I know that I need to keep my intensity level up. I'll go as hard as I can for a while, and then suddenly I find myself just standing there watching. I don't know why, but I'm working on it."

Horton, who hailed from Kershaw, South Carolina, proved to be such a hard-working post defender that Summitt once noted, "As Karla goes, Tennessee goes."

The soft-spoken Horton found the comment a bit overwhelming. "That's really a strong statement," she said. "It puts a lot of pressure on me but it makes me feel good, too. I don't feel I have this great control over the team, but I do feel like I'm a leader."

Spinks, from Forest Hills, Kentucky, was cast from the same mold as Horton—a tough defensive player and rebounder with adequate offensive skills. "I know the other teams don't fear me for my scoring," she said, "but I feel that they have to respect me for my defense. I usually start off strong, and I've been successful at holding the other team's best player down."

Taking turns battling Tech's 6'4" Tori Harrison much as they had on Long Beach's Cindy Brown one game earlier, Frost, Horton, and Spinks limited the towering Techster to 3 field goals in 11 attempts. They also prompted a 47–36 rebounding edge against a Tech team that had dominated the backboards 50–33 in the previous meeting. As a result, the Lady Vols limited the Lady Techsters to 33 percent shooting and 44 points, matching the lowest point total in program history.

The final score—Tennessee 67, Louisiana Tech 44—was so convincing even losing coach Leon Barmore felt obliged to

No Time to Monkey Around

When Pat Summitt showed up for the 1987 NCAA Final Four, she had no chip on her shoulder . . . just a monkey on her back. After seven trips to the Final Four without a title, Tennessee's coach appeared incapable of winning the big one.

Still, she insists she never had any doubts. "I hadn't worried about it one bit, honestly," she said shortly after beating Louisiana Tech in the title game. "To tell the truth, I was pretty confident. I'm a dreamer and a believer, and I believed that we were going to win it."

Incredibly, Richard and Hazel Head missed their eldest daughter's crowning achievement. They were back home in Henrietta, waiting for their youngest daughter, Lynn, to give birth.

praise the victors. "I thought Tennessee played as good a defensive game as I've ever seen," he said. "They forced us out of our offense and obviously did a good job scouting our game Friday night, because we had put in some new stuff for that game."

Frost underscored the point by relating how Tennessee utilized its pregame walk-through drill: "Pat had us practice everything that Tech did on offense in our minds. We were ready."

Even Summitt seemed satisfied with the defensive effort. "We played great defense," she said. "Today, I thought defense could win a championship—and it did."

So, after seven ill-fated trips to the Final Four, the perennial bridesmaids finally stepped to the altar. The "corn-fed chicks" ruled the roost.

Tutu Good to Be True

"I don't know if this is for me." It had taken every ounce of nerve the young woman could muster to walk into the Lady Vol basketball office, take a deep breath, and mutter those eight words. But she had to say them.

After four months in Knoxville, the soft-spoken freshman was convinced she'd made a huge mistake. Pat Summitt's tough-love approach was simply too much "tough" and not enough "love." The player was tired of hearing: "You don't have freshman skills and you don't have a freshman body, so we're not going to treat you like a freshman." She was tired of hearing the harsh words Summitt spewed following a poor performance. The freshman had been so visibly shaken by one postgame tirade that several seniors gathered around her. Yet their words proved less than comforting: "You're going to have to put up with this for four years."

I can't take four years of this, the lanky young woman thought. That's why she stood in the basketball office, spilling her guts to assistant coach Mickie DeMoss, the woman who had worked so hard to recruit her. Whereas Summitt could be stern and intimidating, DeMoss was petite and bubbly, with a soft Southern drawl and a disarmingly sweet smile. As the player finished sharing her concerns about Summitt's rigid coaching style, DeMoss nodded, then offered a few words of encouragement:

"This system works. It worked for a long time before you got here. We've won three national championships. It's going to be tough at times, but this toughness will make you better."

Soothed by DeMoss's soft tone and irrefutable logic, the player's anger began to dissipate. Then the diminutive assistant coach delivered the clincher:

"This is where you want to be, and this is where you *need* to be," she said. "Hang in there."

With a nod, Chamique Holdsclaw turned and walked out of the office. DeMoss watched the player leave, never suspecting that she had just assured Tennessee of three more national championships.

Considered by many to be the greatest player in the history of women's basketball, Holdsclaw would earn All-America recognition in each of her four years as a Lady Vol. She would become the first woman ever to win the Sullivan Award, given annually to the country's premier amateur athlete. All told, she would win more than a hundred awards during her stint in Knoxville. But her development into a world-class athlete started when she was a lanky ten-year-old back in Queens, New York.

One day, as she glided smoothly across the floor, she became almost oblivious to the bodies surrounding her. Though somewhat nervous, she knew the moves she'd been practicing would work if she maintained her focus. This was her stage . . . her moment. Leaving her feet, she spun athletically in midair. She finished, landed as softly as a butterfly, then soaked up the applause of the appreciative crowd. Strolling proudly from the floor, she was greeted by her coach, who offered a pat on the back and a few words of congratulation. Flashing a shy smile, Chamique removed her tutu and her ballet slippers for the ride home from Lincoln Center.

Even before she was making crossover dribbles and fall-away jump shots, Holdsclaw was making leaps and pirouettes for a children's ballet troupe. Her days as an aspiring ballerina would be short-lived, but they helped develop the grace and body control that eventually would make her a household name.

Because she went on to become an Olympian, the number one pick in the Women's National Basketball Association draft, and a millionaire, Holdsclaw is considered to have a charmed life. That hasn't always been the case, however. Only eleven years old when her parents divorced, she was placed in the care of her grandmother, June Holdsclaw. Growing up in Astoria Houses project in Queens, Chamique watched as the crime rate and the mortality rate staged a daily battle for supremacy.

"I can basically say I've seen it all," she recalled of her childhood. "I've seen people doing drugs in front of the Apollo [Theater]. I've seen people get robbed. I've seen people get chased by cops. You're not naive anymore."

As tough as the streets were, June Holdsclaw was even tougher. She imposed strict rules on her granddaughter and rigidly enforced them. She made Chamique go to church. She made her stay home at night and off the streets. She made her do her homework as soon as she arrived home from school. She made her take part in cultural activities, particularly arts and crafts. She made her attend private school when her grades slipped during one ill-fated year at public school. She forbade her to visit friends' homes, insisting Chamique's friends visit her home. She steered her granddaughter toward activities sponsored by the Lutheran Church or the local Boys and Girls Club. "On Saturdays," June said more than once, "you're not going to be hanging around in the streets doing nothing."

Of course, once Chamique discovered a basketball court seventy-three paces from the front door of her grandmother's apartment, "doing nothing" was never an option again.

The lure of the court proved virtually irresistible. At age twelve, headstrong Chamique skipped school three days in a row to work on her game. When she learned of this, June angrily telephoned the New York State Board of Education to ask why she hadn't been notified of the absences. On another occasion, Chamique feigned illness to avoid Sunday church services, then headed for the basketball court while her grandmother worshipped alone. This misdeed got her grounded for two weeks. Chamique called it "overprotective." June called it love.

Chamique was so drawn to the tap, tap, tap of dribbled basketballs and the clang of errant shots bounding off iron rims that she began dropping by the local court every day. Watching the boys play pickup games, she dreamed of a day when they would invite her to join them. When they didn't, she waited patiently until they left, then took the court and tried to copy the skills she'd observed. Finally, after weeks as a frustrated spectator, she got her opportunity to be a participant. The experience forced her to face a harsh reality: She wasn't big enough, strong enough, fast enough, or skilled enough to compete with the guys. Not yet.

So she got bigger, stronger, faster, and more skilled. She began spending five hours per day on the playground court. Sometimes six. Occasionally seven. Every jump shot, every free throw, every spin move brought her one step closer to the level she needed to attain. Classmates at Intermediate School 126 nicknamed her "Flat Leaver" because she would just "flat leave" for the basketball court as soon as school ended, rain or shine. "I would be out playing in the rain," she recalled. "Sometimes, there would be snow on the court."

Her idol was Thurman Holdsclaw, an uncle who had played varsity basketball at Carroll College in Montana. The locals told Chamique her game was very similar to her uncle's, and that made her very proud. She lost a relative and a role model when he died tragically at age twenty-nine in a car crash. "He was the one I always measured myself against," she remembered. "I was devastated when he died."

Chamique continued fine-tuning her game. By age thirteen, she had arrived. She started on the local Boys and Girls Club team ahead of an eleven-year-old boy named Ron Artest, who would go on to star at St. John's University and in the National Basketball Association. Artest took some good-natured kidding about this in later years but accepted the wisecracks graciously. "I didn't mind," he said. "Everyone knew she was the best player on the team."

She also was the best player on the playground—beating the boys at their own game. "When I first got out there, I was actually horrible," she recalled years later. "Nobody wanted to pick me. As I got better, everybody started wanting me."

Young Holdsclaw played a modest role on the team as a freshman at Christ the King High School but still helped it claim the state championship and a top-three national ranking. She hoped to spend the off-season playing for a sixteen-and-under Amateur Athletic Union team, but her high school coach vetoed that plan. Instead, Vincent Cannizzaro placed her on a fourteen-and-under AAU team. He hoped the unassuming Holdsclaw would gain some confidence playing against competition she could dominate. The strategy worked.

"I saw that I was better than those girls," Holdsclaw recalled years later. "That next season I had so much confidence. I had averaged just a little bit of minutes my freshman year, and then I became an instant star."

Her stardom did not surprise her coach. Recognizing the enormity of her potential, Cannizzaro candidly told her: "You have the ability to change the game of women's basketball."

And she did. Holdsclaw led Christ the King to three more state titles and three more top-three national rankings. In the process she scored 2,223 career points, earned All-America recognition three years in a row, and was tabbed National Player of the Year as a senior. During her four varsity seasons, she played in just three losing games. Whenever an opponent began to rally, Holds-claw simply raised her game to another level, single-handedly thwarting the comeback.

"You could always tell when she had taken a game over," Cannizzaro said. "She became more of a presence. She blossomed."

Tennessee's DeMoss witnessed a portion of the blossoming process while attending an AAU tournament in Chattanooga. It's a day she'll never forget. "She just put on a show," DeMoss recalled. "Probably twenty-five coaches were there, and every-body's jaws just dropped open. I thought, 'This kid can play.'"

Upon returning to Knoxville, DeMoss's uncharacteristically glowing report convinced Summitt to make a recruiting visit to Holdsclaw's home in Queens. Their first meeting would prove memorable.

"You look fake," Holdsclaw said mere moments into Summitt's visit.

Conversely, Grandma June found the Lady Vol coach refresh-ingly candid and genuine. When Summitt did not promise Chamique a starting job—only an opportunity to compete for one—June nodded her approval. A native of Alabama, she could relate to another strong Southern woman. When Summitt spoke of the discipline required to be a Lady Vol, June's eyes gleamed. Noting this, DeMoss decided Summitt's tough-as-nails image could be used to Tennessee's advantage. "If you don't go to class, you don't play," the Lady Vol aide noted. "If you don't practice hard, you don't practice any more."

Summitt won over June Holdsclaw on that first visit, but she would have to return several times to win over June's talented granddaughter. Flattery, it seemed, was not going to get her

Living the Dream

Coaches always look for an edge in recruiting, and Tennessee coach Pat Summitt found a dandy during her pursuit of New York City superstar Chamique Holdsclaw in the winter of 1995.

Holdsclaw's favorite quote was "Don't dream it. Be it." Upon learning this tidbit, Summitt had the quote engraved on a small plate, which she hung above one of the lockers in Tennessee's palatial dressing room. Summitt made sure Holdsclaw saw that locker when she made her official visit to Knoxville later that winter.

The ploy worked. Holdsclaw signed with Tennessee and drew inspiration from that quote before each home game. Never content merely to pursue a dream, she always sought to live it. And as soon as one dream became a reality, she moved on to the next one. "Once I accomplish my goal, I raise it to another level," she explained. "If you're content where you are, you won't get anywhere."

No player in the history of women's basketball has faced more gadget defenses than Holdsclaw. No player has had to overcome more pushing, jostling, and holding. No player has had to deal with more pressure to be "on" every minute of every game. Through it all, Holdsclaw somehow maintained an amazingly high performance level.

"It's about pride, wanting to be the best," she once said. "If I'm tired, I just look at my opponent. She's as tired as I am. I just look at her and get a burst of energy. I may be dying, but I look at her and suck it up."

anywhere with Chamique Holdsclaw. "When I was recruiting her I kept mentioning Cheryl Miller," Summitt recalled, referring to the former Southern Cal superstar. "She kept telling me, 'I don't want to be Cheryl Miller. I want to be Chamique Holdsclaw.'"

Between Summitt's persistence, DeMoss's sales pitch, and a nudge from Grandma June, the young superstar eventually decided to sign with Tennessee. Chamique's decision proved heartbreaking for dozens of rival recruiters. "I always say the good ones will find you," Summitt noted. "She found *everyone*."

Because women's basketball was still a relatively obscure sport in 1995, Holdsclaw's arrival on The Hill created only a mild stir. Her collegiate debut did little to increase the stir. Clearly nervous, the 6'2" forward sank just 5 of 16 field-goal attempts en route to 13 points in a 78–51 blitz of Virginia. She scored 11 points in Game 2 and 13 more in Game 3. It wasn't until the Lady Vols traveled to the Kona Basketball Classic in Kailua-Kona, Hawaii, that Holdsclaw began to live up to her sterling reputation. She hit 13 of 16 shots and scored 27 points as Tennessee blasted Purdue 81–63 in the tourney semifinals, then added 16 more as the Lady Vols tripped Penn State 79–67 in the title game. Those performances earned her Most Valuable Player honors and high praise from Lady Lion coach Rene Portland. "Holdsclaw makes them such a good team," Portland said. "She's an incredible dominator."

Not always. Holdsclaw scored 15 points in a Game 13 loss to Connecticut but made only one basket in the final twelve minutes. When Summitt grumbled that she needed to be more assertive at crunch time, Holdsclaw responded by recording 21 points and 19 rebounds against Georgia in Tennessee's very next game.

At Tennessee Holdsclaw rose above the rest.
Randy Moore/Rocky Top News

Worth Her Weight in Points

During her four-year varsity career, Chamique Holdsclaw averaged 20.4 points per game. The way Lady Vol head coach Pat Summitt saw it, that gave her a value of roughly 40 points per game. Summitt figured Holdsclaw's presence was always worth an additional 20 points per game just because of the positive impact she had on her teammates.

"That's 20 points I wouldn't be able to get out of our team," the coach said, "no matter how long and hard I made them practice."

Another defining moment came in Game 19 against top-ranked Louisiana Tech, when the resilient rookie recorded 23 points and 13 rebounds in a 77–72 victory. Tech coach Leon Barmore was so impressed he called Holdsclaw "possibly the best freshman to ever play the game. . . . She hit some incredible shots. When you do that, you have greatness written on you." Even the slow-to-praise Summitt chimed in: "We've not had a freshman impact this program in my career like her." Days later, ESPN tabbed Holdsclaw its National Player of the Week, the first female so honored in the award's six-year existence.

Holdsclaw finished the regular season with averages of 16.9 points and 9.7 rebounds per game, earning Southeastern Conference Freshman of the Year and first-team all-conference recognition. Just as everything seemed to be falling into place, she injured her right knee in the first half of the SEC Tournament's title game between Tennessee and Alabama. Writhing in pain, she had to be helped from the floor. "My heart dropped down to my toes," senior guard Michelle Marciniak said. "I got really scared for her."

In the first five minutes after Holdsclaw left the lineup, Alabama outscored Tennessee 14–2, turning a 19–8 deficit into a 22–21 lead. Summitt called a timeout at this point and tried to turn Holdsclaw's loss into a psychological boost. "Chamique wants an SEC championship ring," the coach said. "She's done an awful lot for you, so let's go get her a ring."

The Lady Vols did just that, struggling mightily but eventually prevailing 64–60. "Our coaching staff always wondered what our team would do without Chamique," Summitt mused. "We found out tonight, and it wasn't pretty."

Despite a partial tear of the medial collateral ligament, Holdsclaw never missed a game. Fighting through the pain, she led Tennessee to the NCAA championship game, where she capped her freshman season by scoring 16 points and grabbing 14 rebounds in an 83–65 defeat of Georgia.

Although the Lady Vols struggled through an unusually poor 1996–97 regular season—going 23–10 and placing fifth in the Southeastern Conference standings—they jelled at tournament time. With Holdsclaw leading the way, Tennessee shocked unbeaten Connecticut in the Midwest Region finals at Iowa City, then trounced Notre Dame in the Final Four semifinals. The Lady Vols trailed Old Dominion 49–47 in the NCAA championship game, but Holdsclaw sparked a 12–2 spurt that sent Tennessee on its way to a 68–59 victory and a second consecutive national title.

Holdsclaw took the title in stride. It's no wonder. She won the New York City championship as an eighth-grader, then won state championships as a freshman, sophomore, junior, and senior. Winning national titles in her first two years of college meant that she had ended seven consecutive basketball seasons with a championship-game victory. When a sportswriter pointed out that she didn't know how it felt to end a season with a loss, Holdsclaw quipped, "No, and I don't *want* to know."

She wouldn't find out in 1997–98. It proved to be a magical time in Lady Vol history, and Holdsclaw was the featured magician. She scored a career-high 37 points in a 99–60 blitz of Florida, then single-handedly outscored Georgia's entire team 22–21 in the first half of another blowout victory. Louisiana Tech coach Leon Barmore called her "the best player, in my opinion, who has ever played this game."

After guiding Tennessee through a 33–0 regular season, Holdsclaw somehow shifted into an even higher gear—increasing her scoring average from 23.5 to 25.2 and her rebounding average from 8.4 to 9.7 during the postseason. She recorded 25 points in the NCAA championship game, a 93–75 pasting of Louisiana Tech that capped a 39–0 season and produced an unprecedented third straight national title.

"When the playoffs come, I'm happy," she gushed. "I'm excited. Everything's on the line. That's like going to play in the park. If you're going to play against the best, you better come ready. If you don't, everybody's going to laugh at you."

No one was laughing at Chamique Holdsclaw, but everyone in women's basketball was watching her. A three-time All-American with three national titles to her credit, she seemingly had no worlds left to conquer. With a reported $10 million in potential endorsements awaiting her, would she forgo her senior season and turn pro?

Struggling with the decision, Chamique returned to Queens to ask her beloved grandmother if she should return for her final year of college. The answer was not surprising. "I've never asked you for anything," June said, "but that's the only thing I want you to do."

Actually, there was *another* thing June wanted Chamique to do—continue honoring the rules of the house. Returning to Queens that summer, Chamique twice stayed out until 2:00 A.M. It didn't matter that she was a three-time All-American and a three-time NCAA champion. "Young lady," June chastised, "you *still* have a curfew." For the remainder of the summer, Chamique was home by 12:30. Sharp.

Just as Grandma June continued making her toe the line back in Astoria, Summitt continued making Chamique toe the line in Knoxville. After three years of the head coach's strict discipline, Holdsclaw finally came to respect Summitt's no-nonsense approach. One time, taking the seat next to her head coach on the team bus, Chamique said: "I just finished your book [*Reach for the Summit*], and I finally understand you."

Summitt's reaction? "I should have written it two years ago."

Finally at peace with her coach, Holdsclaw opened her senior year much as she began her previous college seasons. She continued to wear jersey number 23—a tribute to the 23rd Psalm, "The Lord is my shepherd, I shall not want . . ." She continued to write motivational notes on her socks, such as "Focus" and "Rebound." And she continued to showcase the

Upstaging the Coach

With six NCAA championships and an Olympic gold medal on her coaching résumé, Pat Summitt is generally considered the most famous name in women's basketball. But even she had to take a back seat during the late 1990s.

On a recruiting trip during the 1998–99 season, Summitt met a woman who happened to be a diehard women's basketball fan. Recognizing the high-profile coach, the woman asked her young son if he wanted an autograph from the lady who had guided Tennessee to three consecutive NCAA titles.

"No, I don't need hers," the youngster replied. "I have Chamique Holdsclaw's autograph."

Summitt's ego took another hit on a subsequent recruiting trip. This time a young boy asked for the coach's autograph, then stipulated that she also sign Holdsclaw's name next to her own.

most dazzling skills in women's basketball, attracting record-breaking crowds wherever she went.

"People like to watch her play," Summitt noted. "There's poise in her game. When you watch Chamique, you are watching a very graceful and talented player, a do-it-all player. She can make the very difficult seem easy."

Incredibly, this ability to make the miraculous appear mundane led some observers to see Holdsclaw as a slacker whose effort level never quite matched her talent level. "A lot of people look at that and say, 'Boy, she's not playing hard,'" Summitt conceded. "But that's just because she's always under control. She's so efficient that it doesn't look like she's working hard. But then you look at the numbers at the end of the game—she's the leading scorer and rebounder again."

Holdsclaw passed Bridgette Gordon to become the program's all-time leading scorer with a 24-point effort against Arkansas just one month into her senior season of 1998–99. She hit 12 of 17 floor shots and totaled 25 points in a 92–81 upset of top-ranked Connecticut. She produced 33 points and 15 rebounds in a 95–79 win at number-four Georgia. Shortly thereafter, she became the Southeastern Conference's all-time scoring leader with a 22-point effort against Georgia in the league tournament. Saving her best for last, she scored a new career high of 39 points in her final home appearance, an 89–62 rout of Boston College in the NCAA East subregional.

Although she ultimately guided Tennessee to a 31–3 record, Holdsclaw's bid for a fourth consecutive national title fell short. Plagued by some key injuries, the Lady Vols lost the NCAA championship game to Duke by a 69–63 score. Still, Holdsclaw's legacy was secure. She ended her college career with more points (3,025) and more rebounds (1,295) than anyone who ever played at Tennessee, male or female. A star on the court, she was a celebrity off the court. She had graced the cover of *TV Guide*, been featured on *60 Minutes*, and been profiled by *Time* magazine. She had given more than seven hundred interviews during her senior season alone. Still, she found time to enhance her reputation as the greatest female basketball player of her era— maybe the greatest of *any* era.

Holdsclaw sheepishly accepts the Sullivan Award and Pat Summitt's applause.
Randy Moore/Rocky Top News

Ultimately, the same woman that nearly ran her off as a Lady Vol freshman would be entrusted with putting Holdsclaw's remarkable career in perspective.

"I've never had a player like Chamique," Summitt mused. "I don't think anyone has."

As Good as It Gets: 39-0

Semeka Randall didn't need a crystal ball, tarot cards, or tea leaves to foresee a bright future for the 1997–98 Tennessee Lady Vols. All she needed was a few preseason workouts with fellow freshmen Tamika Catchings, Ace Clement, and Teresa Geter, plus an up-close look at returning superstar Chamique Holdsclaw.

Holdsclaw already was being hailed as the greatest player in the history of women's basketball. Catchings was being hailed as the next Holdsclaw. Clement was a slick point guard who had broken the Philadelphia high school scoring record of National Basketball Association Hall of Famer Wilt Chamberlain. Geter was a talented post player with a knack for blocking shots and spearing rebounds. Randall could see greatness in her class-mates and in herself. A perpetual motion machine, she seemed equally adept at energizing her team's offense and disrupting the opposing team's offense.

As Randall walked off the floor following a particularly taxing preseason practice, a reporter approached her. Not surprisingly, his question concerned the celebrated "Fab Four" freshman class. No big shock there; it seemed *every* question concerned the Fab Four. But that was fine with Randall. She envisioned greatness for the group and had no reservations about sharing her vision.

"We have a powerhouse," she said, flashing the charismatic grin that would become her trademark. "We're going to have a phenomenal year. We're going to have up-and-down, 94-feet basketball getting the crowd into it. It's going to be a rah-rah year."

Such an outrageous outburst could be chalked up to the exuberance of youth, except for one detail: Randall's forecast made the prophecy of Nostradamus look like a parlor trick. Every word proved to be deadly accurate. If anything, the season ahead would prove even more incredible than her forecast.

Opening night saw 6,602 fans show up at Thompson-Boling Arena to see first-hand if the Fab Four was all it was cracked up to be. They did not leave disappointed. Randall hit 10 of 12 floor shots, scored a game-high 24 points, and caused many of Ole Miss's 28 turnovers as the Lady Vols romped 92–54.

Game 2 found Tennessee matched against Louisiana Tech, which returned all five starters from a team that whipped the Lady Vols twice the previous season. The Lady Techsters appeared on the verge of another victory, leading 50–45 midway through the second half, but the Fab Four had other ideas. With Holdsclaw taking a breather on the bench, the rambunctious rookies spearheaded a 12–0 run that produced a 57–50 lead and, eventually, a 75–61 triumph.

"This is a special class," Lady Vol assistant Mickie DeMoss mused. "A *very* special class."

The 2–0 start moved to 3–0, then 4–0. Game 5 was projected to be Tennessee's most difficult challenge to date, however. The Lady Vols hit the road to face Stanford, which had a 49-game home winning streak and had pounded the Lady Vols by 18 points on their previous trip to the West Coast two years earlier.

The outlook did not look promising as the Cardinal shot 56.7 percent from the field en route to a 45–44 halftime lead. Fortunately for Tennessee, the "Three Meeks" (so named for the middle syllable of their first names) sparked a huge comeback. Chamique Holdsclaw scored 25 points, Tamika Catchings 20, and Semeka Randall 17 as the Lady Vols outscored Stanford 44–25 in the second half and romped 88–70.

Randall, playing her first big road game, clearly was not intimidated. "If you love to compete," she said, "it shouldn't matter where we're at. Just go out and kick butt."

A new foot did the butt-kicking in Tennessee's Game 6 victory at Portland. Little-used long-range bomber Misty Greene came off the bench to score 16 points in a 74–51 romp. With the Lady Vols clinging to a modest 42–32 second-half lead, Greene nailed 3 three-pointers that helped boost the lead from 10 points to 22.

Days later, Holdsclaw returned to her New York City roots when Tennessee competed in the Big Apple Classic. She looked right at home, earning Most Valuable Player recognition after

The Fab Four: Tamika Catchings and Teresa Geter (kneeling), Ace Clement and Semeka Randall (standing). Randy Moore/Rocky Top News

scoring 24 points in a 93–61 trouncing of George Mason and 12 more in a 78–28 drubbing of Manhattan College.

"God has blessed her with great talents," Randall told the assembled media.

"Thank you, Sister Randall," Holdsclaw replied, grinning impishly.

"Amen."

Lightheartedness was a new emotion for Holdsclaw, who had done some serious brooding the previous season. Now that high-scoring freshmen Catchings and Randall had lifted some of the burden from her slender shoulders, Holdsclaw found both her game and her mood elevated.

"I'm so much more relaxed," she explained. "I know I have to play hard, but it's not like last year, when we'd be down by 10 points and my teammates would look at me for five straight possessions. Teams can guard me tight, but Tamika and Semeka can slip in there and score now."

Still, the fun and games nearly came to a screeching halt in Game 10. Fifth-ranked Illinois roared to a 22-point first-half bulge and led by 18 early in the second half. Tennessee's full-court pressure turned the tide at this point, however, producing 12 turnovers in an eight-minute explosion during which the Lady Vols outscored the Illini 32–5 and turned a 48–30 deficit into a 62–53 lead. Catchings finished with 20 points and Holdsclaw 19 as Tennessee prevailed 78–68. The same duo was at it again in Game 14: Holdsclaw registered 28 points and Catching 24 as the Lady Vols trounced visiting Arkansas 88–58.

January 3 would prove to be a watershed day for women's basketball. The biggest crowd in the history of the game—24,597 strong—jammed into Thompson-Boling Arena to watch top-ranked Tennessee host third-ranked Connecticut and its fifty-two-game regular-season winning streak. Down by 17 early, the Huskies pulled within a point at 49–48 midway through the second half. But Randall forced a turnover and Kellie Jolly nailed a three-pointer to shift the momentum back to Tennessee. Randall finished with 25 points, and the Lady Vols finished with an 84–69 victory.

Showing she could still dominate a game if the mood struck her, Holdsclaw scored outside, inside, and in-between — 37 points in all — as Tennessee thrashed Florida 99–60 and moved to 17–0. Fueled by a 21–0 outburst, the Lady Vols built a 52–18 halftime lead. Even the hard-to-please Summitt was satisfied, calling the spurt "as fine a basketball as I think anyone could expect a team to play for an extended period of time." Florida's Carol Ross was impressed with the Lady Vols, too, noting: "They're quicker at every position. . . . If you can't catch 'em, you can't stop 'em."

Holdsclaw, Catchings, and Randall continued to win games and influence people. Even DeMoss was moved to shake her head in amazement. "We'll never see another team quite like this one," she said. "We're going to spoil our fans."

Holdsclaw scored a season-low 8 points in Game 20 versus DePaul, but it hardly mattered. Her teammates took up the slack — and then some. Freshmen Catchings (35 points), Randall (18), and Geter (18) provided enough punch to power a 125–46 annihilation. The dynamic Lady Vols scored the game's first 21 points and coasted from there. "Our basketball team came out on fire," Summitt said. "Tamika Catchings was all-world, very explosive."

Moments after an 86–54 trouncing of ninth-ranked Vanderbilt improved Tennessee's record to 21–0, Summitt admitted being the Lady Vols' number-one fan, as well as their head coach: "If I wasn't on the bench, I'd be in the stands. I'd pay money to watch these kids play. They're exciting. They can do a lot of things I haven't seen many collegiate teams do, as far as the pace they play at."

Gradually, the whispers of an unbeaten season became a roar. Then the Alabama Crimson Tide came to town for Game 23. Realizing his team couldn't run with Tennessee, Bama coach Rick Moody decided to see if the Lady Vols could walk with the Tide. Slowing the game's pace to a crawl, Alabama pushed Tennessee physically and emotionally before bowing 73–66. The Tide became the first opponent to play Tennessee to a single-digit loss.

Even in victory, the Lady Vols suffered a major loss. Sophomore guard Kyra Elzy, the team's unquestioned defensive stopper, suffered a torn anterior cruciate ligament midway through the first half that would end her season.

When Old Dominion's third-ranked Lady Monarchs showed up at Thompson-Boling Arena on February 8, a crowd of 20,495 came along with them. They were eyewitnesses as Randall stole the show—and the ball—all evening long. The mercurial freshman recorded 6 steals and forced All-America guard Ticha Penicheiro into 9 turnovers and 3–of–15 shooting as the Lady Vols rolled 85–61.

"Semeka has a passion for defense," Summitt noted moments after her team moved to 25–0. "To find that in a high school or college player, you've got something really special."

Analyzing the game for ESPN2, former ODU superstar Nancy Lieberman-Cline called the Lady Vols "the best team I've ever seen. . . . It's just unbelievable how good they are, and it's great for women's basketball."

As the Fab Four freshman class continued taking the hoops world by storm, something downright incredible happened: Holdsclaw occasionally drifted into the background. Every once in a

The Definite Dozen

You could call them Coach's Commandments. You could call them Pat's Principles. You could call them Summitt's Suggestions. Or you could call them the "Definite Dozen," as the ultra-successful coach of Tennessee's Lady Vol basketball team does.

Whatever you call them, the twelve directives Pat Summitt lives by have helped Tennessee register more than 800 victories during her illustrious career.

1. Respect. Yourself and others.
2. Take full responsibility.
3. Develop and demonstrate loyalty.
4. Learn to be a great communicator.
5. Discipline yourself so no one else has to.
6. Make hard work your passion.
7. Don't just work hard. Work smart.
8. Put the team before yourself.
9. Make winning an attitude.
10. Be a competitor.
11. Change is a must.
12. Handle success like you handle failure.

while, though, she'd remind everyone why many observers labeled her the greatest ever to play the women's game. February 14 against Auburn was one of those times.

Holdsclaw nailed 15 of 21 floor shots en route to a career-high 39 points as Tennessee clipped the Lady Tigers 79–63. Joe Ciampi, who had made three appearances in the national championship game during nearly two decades as Auburn's head coach, could only shake his head in amazement. "I've been doing this for nineteen years," he said, "and this is a team that scares you in trying to prepare for, because they're on a level that we all fantasize about."

The fantasy season continued with a 90–58 drubbing of Louisiana State University that gave Tennessee a 30–0 record and the first unbeaten regular season in program history. The Lady Vols hit 13 of their first 16 field-goal tries and forced 15 turnovers in the opening eight minutes on the way to a 32–8 lead. "The game was basically over after the first three minutes," losing coach Sue Gunter mused.

Not for Laurie Milligan. Summitt had penciled her into the "Senior Day" starting lineup, despite a degenerative condition in her left knee that had limited her to one cameo appearance in the previous twenty-nine regular-season games. Milligan was so energized she registered 4 points, 3 assists, and 3 steals—all in eleven minutes of inspired play.

When the final horn sounded, the Lady Vols could celebrate the most remarkable regular season in program history. They had won their thirty regular-season games by an average of 31.1 points. Incredibly, they had fared even better against rugged Southeastern Conference opposition, winning their fourteen league tests by an average of 32 points.

"I don't see anybody in the country that can touch this team," Gunter said.

Apparently, she hadn't seen Alabama. Having played Tennessee to a 7-point loss in the regular-season meeting at Knoxville, Crimson Tide players were confident they could crash the Lady Vols' party at the Southeastern Conference Tournament. Bama even got an assist from the national media, when *Sports Illustrated* published a cover story on Summitt's program.

Asked if the infamous "*SI* cover jinx" concerned her, the Lady Vol coach emphatically shook her head. "Not with this group," she replied.

Still, the Lady Vols appeared ripe for an upset. Their path to the national title was littered with question marks: Could they stay healthy? Could they meet the challenge of winning a third consecutive NCAA title? Could they handle the pressure of preserving a perfect record? Could they remain hungry in the wake of a 30–0 regular season? Could they maintain in March the amazing energy level they had exhibited in November, December, January, and February? Finally, as the most celebrated team in women's basketball history, could they avoid tripping over their own hype? That task grew more daunting as coaches throughout the country continued to shower the team with glowing tributes.

"I really feel that if you put Holdsclaw, Catchings, and Randall on three different teams, you'd have three top-10 teams," Vanderbilt's Jim Foster said. "The fact they have all three of them is frightening."

Arkansas coach Gary Blair went a step further: "I think the SEC is getting a bad rap. They think the SEC is down this year. The SEC is *not* down. Tennessee is on a different planet this year."

Even Summitt, who already had coached five national championship teams, singled out her latest edition as something special. "When this team gets on a run," she said, "they can steamroll you very quickly."

Tennessee proved as much in the Southeastern Conference Tournament semifinals. After building a 61–29 halftime lead against Vanderbilt, the Lady Vols could have coasted home from there. Instead, they blitzed the Commodores 32–2 to open the second half en route to a 106–45 annihilation. "They're redefining the game of women's basketball," Vandy's Foster surmised, less than amused by his role in the milestone.

Alabama's Moody had to smile at such talk. The more Tennessee's players bought into the hyperbole, the more likely they were to walk blindly into an ambush when they faced his Crimson Tide the following afternoon in the tournament finals.

Moody's game plan was fiendishly simple: He'd offset Tennessee's quickness by forcing a slow tempo, and he'd neutralize Tennessee's athleticism by turning the game into a brawl. If Bama could accomplish these two objectives, it could keep the score close enough that the Tide would have a chance to win in the final minutes. And that's exactly what happened.

After scoring 106 points the night before, Tennessee managed just 8 points in the first seven minutes against Bama. A 10–0 spurt turned an 11–8 deficit into an 18–11 lead, but Alabama closed to 18–15. Another mini-surge enabled the Lady Vols to pull ahead 29–19, but the Tide scored the final 7 points of the half and trailed just 29–26 at the break.

Alabama whittled the lead to 37–36 early in the second half, but a three-pointer by Clement helped fuel a 20–7 spurt that gave Tennessee a seemingly safe 57–43 lead with 6:02 to play. Bama wouldn't go away, however. Brittney Ezell, a native Tennessean who had been snubbed by Lady Vol recruiters, hit two baskets, and brawny Tausha Mills muscled home a layup. Suddenly, Tennessee's lead had been whittled to 63–58 with 41.9 seconds remaining.

Tennessee fans squirmed in their seats. They weren't accustomed to late-game tension. The Lady Vols weren't, either, but they adapted. Catchings drained a pair of free throws; then fellow freshman Randall scored on a driving layup as Tennessee hung on for a 67–63 triumph.

"Their physical play really caught us off guard," Summitt said of the Tide. "And we had some people who, emotionally and mentally, were not at the same level they were last night."

Although Alabama failed to win, the Tide succeeded in shattering Tennessee's aura of invincibility. Though still unbeaten, the Lady Vols no longer appeared unbeatable.

"Mentally and emotionally, we have to be a lot stronger," Summitt said. "We can't be afraid to go out and win. When you're ranked number one and you're undefeated, the hardest thing to do is what you're *supposed* to do."

The Lady Vols did precisely what they were supposed to do in the NCAA Tournament's Mideast subregional, methodically mauling Liberty 102–58 and Western Kentucky 82–62 to earn a berth in the region semifinals at Nashville.

After two uninspired defensive efforts in the subregional, Randall bounced back with a vengeance in Music City. Her quick hands and quicker feet forced Rutgers guards Natasha Pointer (9) and Tomora Young (8) into 17 turnovers as the Lady Vols romped 92–60. In addition to her defensive dominance, Randall scored 17 points and grabbed a game-high 13 rebounds. The other Meeks didn't do too badly, either: Holdsclaw recorded 25 points and Catchings 23.

As happened after the Vanderbilt game, however, Tennessee followed a superior performance with a sloppy one. Stumbling and bumbling their way through the first thirty-two minutes of the region finals, the Lady Vols trailed North Carolina 61–49 with 7:16 remaining. A prohibitively pro-Tennessee crowd feared the worst but hoped for the best—another of the Lady Vols' patented eruptions. That's precisely what occurred.

Point guard Kellie Jolly provided a steadying influence for the volatile 1997–98 title team.

Randy Moore/Rocky Top News

Geter, the most obscure member of the Fab Four freshman class, got motivated, then got busy. She sandwiched a three-point play and a short jump shot around a couple of Holdsclaw free throws as Tennessee closed to 61–56. "She was excited, and I've never seen that side of her," Holdsclaw noted. "She was really pumped."

So was Holdsclaw, who scored 6 points in a span of 16 seconds. Two free throws narrowed the deficit to 62–60 with 5:07 remaining. After intercepting a pass in backcourt, she drove for the game-tying layup at the 5:00 mark. Randall stole the ensuing inbounds attempt and quickly passed to Holdsclaw, who glided through traffic for a layup that gave Tennessee a 64–62 lead with 4:51 to play. Carolina rallied to go up 67–66 with 2:57 to go, but Holdsclaw hit 6 free throws down the stretch to seal a 76–70 Lady Vol victory.

"I didn't want to go out there and lose with all of those people yelling for us," she said. "They probably missed work to come to this game."

The Fab Four had come up big in Tennessee's biggest game to date. Randall finished with 20 points, 8 rebounds, and 3 steals. Catchings added 11 points, 7 rebounds, 3 assists, and 4 steals. Geter hit all 4 field-goal tries, all 3 free throw tries, and speared 8 rebounds. Clement played thirty minutes at the point, helping ignite Tennessee's frantic rally.

Holdsclaw scored 14 points in the game's final 7:06 and finished with 29 for the night. Still, the performance was not one of her better ones. She sank just 8 of 26 field-goal tries and committed 4 turnovers. Fellow junior Jolly also struggled in the region final, prompting Summitt to make a surprising observation: "I think they really felt a lot of responsibility to get this team to Kansas City. Looking at the numbers, the freshmen were ready to play. They had no fear."

Although the rookies played with no fear in the regionals, they showed a bit of anxiety once they reached the Final Four. Facing SEC rival Arkansas in the semifinals, Tennessee clung to a scant 36–28 lead with mere seconds left in the first half. A clutch three-pointer at the buzzer by Jolly boosted the lead to 39–28 at the break.

The Lady Vols were a different team at the start of the second half. A 13–1 burst widened the lead to 52–29, and Tennessee went on to win 86–58. The 28-point victory margin was a Final Four semifinal record.

Moments after scoring 23 points to pace the victory, Holdsclaw stammered when asked what Summitt said at halftime to spark such a dramatic turnaround. "In the locker room, Coach . . . uh . . . Coach . . . uh . . . I think she got on us about . . . uh . . ." Finally, Holdsclaw turned to her coach with a quizzical look and mumbled, "What *was* it you said?"

With a shake of her head, Summitt replied: "I'm not going to bail you out."

Ultimately, the "bail-out" role fell to Jolly. Two nights later in the NCAA title game against Louisiana Tech, she helped Tennessee race to a 55–32 halftime lead. Then, when the Lady Techsters clawed their way back into the game at 72–54, Jolly nailed two long-range three-pointers that boosted the Lady Vols' lead to 76–54 with 11:10 remaining.

"Any hope we had in this game, those two Kellie Jolly 3s ended it," Tech coach Leon Barmore conceded. "I really admire that kid."

So did Summitt, who recalled telling Jolly to "be more aggressive tonight and step up your offensive game" shortly before tipoff. "That's all I had to say," the coach added. "She was taking NBA 3s."

And *making* them. Jolly sank 7 of 10 floor shots, including 4 of 5 from beyond the three-point arc, en route to a career-high 20

Charismatic Semeka Randall was the emotional leader in Tennessee's magical 39–0 season.
Randy Moore/Rocky Top News

points. She also directed the offense nearly flawlessly, committing just 2 turnovers in thirty-four minutes at the point. Although Catchings had scored 27 points and Holdsclaw 25, the media horde headed for Jolly's cubicle in the postgame locker room. Beaming, she was quick to share the credit with her high-profile teammates. "I've got some athletic players surrounding me," she said, "and they're very flashy and fun to watch. I just do my job."

Apparently, her job was to guide Tennessee to a 39–0 record and a third consecutive national title. If so, mission accomplished.

Gracious in defeat, Barmore called the Lady Vols "the greatest women's basketball team I personally have ever seen. They earned it. They worked hard. When it came time to get it done, they got it done."

Indeed they did. That's why school officials were determined to honor them upon their return to Knoxville. A suitable celebration was planned for Thompson-Boling Arena, where the team's historic season had begun four months earlier. Lady Vol coaches Summitt, DeMoss, Holly Warlick, and Al Brown showed up in white Mercedes, gifts of the university. Tennessee's players showed up in stretch limousines. As for the fans . . . well, they showed up in droves.

Women's athletics director Joan Cronan greeted the grateful throng, made a few opening remarks, and then praised the triumphant Lady Vols and their coaches. "Thirty-nine and oh," she said. "Six national championships. And a three-peat. What else could we want?"

Thumbs tucked and fingers upraised, fans shouted their reply: "Four!"

Cardiac Unrest

Sometimes an abundance of willpower can overcome a shortage of star power. That's the only way to explain the remarkable run made by the 2003–04 Tennessee Lady Vols.

With time-out on the floor, Pat Summitt glanced at the Louisiana Superdome scoreboard. It showed Louisiana State and Tennessee tied at 50 with 6 seconds left in their 2004 Final Four semifinal. As the Lady Vols huddled around their coach, their low-key

You've Come a Long Way, Baby

The growth of women's basketball during the past thirty years has been remarkable, and nowhere is that growth more evident than at the University of Tennessee.

In 1974, when Pat Head was hired as head coach, the job was considered a part-time position. By 2004 it had become a year-round endeavor that included summer camps, endorsements, and speaking engagements.

In 1974 Head's salary was a minuscule $250 per month. Her 2004 salary was $824,500, meaning she made more money per hour ($282.25 based on a forty-hour workweek) than she once did per month.

In 1974 Head's only assistance came from Doug Pease, a janitor who voluntarily helped her prepare the gym for home games. The head coach now has a staff of three full-time aides, a graduate assistant, and several administrative aides.

In 1974 the program sold doughnuts to help pay for uniforms and travel expenses. Thirty years later it realizes a profit of roughly $800,000 per year.

In 1974 Tennessee's players traveled to road games in vans, playing mostly in-state opponents located within easy driving distance. In

composure provided a stark contrast to the high-decibel chaos surrounding them. With a colossal victory seemingly imminent, Lady Tiger backers whipped themselves into such a deafening frenzy that Summitt was forced to shout her defensive instructions so she could be heard above the din of the crowd.

As play resumed, LSU inbounded the ball to mercurial mighty-mite Temeka Johnson. Tennessee immediately double-

recent years the team has traveled to Hawaii, Alaska, Belgium, Puerto Rico, France, Switzerland, Italy, and Greece—by jet, of course.

In 1974 the team played its home games in 3,000-seat Alumni Memorial Gym before crowds that could be counted on your fingers and toes. Now it plays in 24,000-seat Thompson-Boling Arena before crowds that sometimes pack the house. Incredibly, the Lady Vols routinely draw more fans to their practices than they once attracted to their games.

All of this is mind-boggling, even for the woman who helped bring about these dramatic changes. "What has happened to this program," Pat Head Summitt said, "I never envisioned."

She may never have envisioned the evolution but she, more than anyone else, caused it. In fact, Summitt has done more than anyone to transform women's basketball from club sport to big-time entertainment over the past three decades. Her devotion to the sport is unsurpassed, which is why she scoffs when asked about leaving to coach in the men's game.

"My whole thinking on that line is that you have an opportunity during your time on Earth to make a difference for women," she said. "What would it matter if you made a difference for men? It's not like they need it."

teamed her. With the game's final seconds slipping away, Johnson tried desperately to escape the trap. In her haste, she lost control of the basketball, which squirted across the floor. Scooping up the loose ball, Tennessee's Shyra Ely spotted LaToya Davis near the basket. Shoveling the ball to her teammate, Ely watched as Davis banked home a layup with 1.2 seconds left to give the Lady Vols a heart-stopping 52–50 victory.

The Cardiac Corps had done it again.

For the third time in as many games, Tennessee had scored in the game's final 2 seconds to eke out a 2-point victory. While the last-second defeat of LSU was just another day at the office for the steel-nerved Lady Vols, it was a bit more taxing for their emotionally drained coach. "This team has low blood pressure," Summitt mused following the fantastic finish. "My blood pressure right now . . . you would not even want to check it."

Three thrillers in a span of nine days will do that to you. The fact the Lady Vols emerged victorious in each of them, earning a berth in the national title game, was a testament more to their will than their skill. "I guess the way we feel is that we're supposed to be here," Ely said, "because we keep finding ways to win."

Unlikely ways to win, to be precise. For the Lady Vols to pull out three consecutive games on their final possession represented an amazing accomplishment. "I'm glad they had another one in them," Summitt said, shaking her head in amazement. "How many postseason games have I got . . . a hundred and one? I would say out of a hundred and one, the last three were the toughest."

And, quite possibly, the sweetest. That's because the 2003–04 Lady Vols had no business making the Final Four, let alone the title game. This was a team that had no star and no point guard. What this squad did have was a level of determination that defied description.

Five months earlier, when Summitt assembled the team for its first day of preseason drills, she did not see a Chamique Holdsclaw, a Tamika Catchings, or a Semeka Randall. She didn't even see a Kara Lawson or a Gwen Jackson, the cornerstones of her 2002–03 squad. Previous Lady Vol rosters represented a *Who's Who* of women's basketball; this one was more "Who's she?":

At 6'5", Ashley Robinson stood tall, literally and competitively, for the 2003–04 Lady Vols.
UT Women's Media Relations

- Ely, a 6'2" junior, was the top returning scorer at just 9.8 points per game. She had done a nice job complementing Lawson and Jackson the previous year but had given no indication she could fill the role of go-to player.
- Ashley Robinson, a 6'5" senior who had been hampered by knee problems throughout her college career, was coming off a junior season in which she shot just 41.8 percent from the field and averaged a paltry 5.8 points per game.
- Tasha Butts entered her senior season with a career field-goal percentage of 35.3 and a career scoring average of 5.1.
- Davis, a perennial backup, had averaged just six minutes and 2.2 points per game as a junior.
- Senior forward Courtney McDaniel, another career backup, was an undersized post player at an even 6'.
- Junior guard Brittany Jackson was known more for her beauty queen looks than her basketball skills.
- Junior Loree Moore, though a solid performer, faced the imposing task of assuming the playmaker/team leader role vacated by Lawson.
- Tye'sha Fluker, a 6'4" sophomore, was coming off a nondescript freshman season that saw her average 3.1 points and 2.5 rebounds while playing ten minutes per game.
- Sophomore Shanna Zolman was a streaky shooter whose defense and ballhandling needed considerable work.
- Sidney Spencer and Dominique Redding were relatively unheralded freshmen who projected to be a year away from contributing significantly.

These eleven players would comprise a 2003–04 squad that appeared destined for mediocrity. Of course, mediocrity is a relative term. By Lady Vol standards, it means winning fewer than thirty games and falling short of the Final Four.

Tennessee certainly didn't look like a Final Four team in the first half of Game 5 at Stanford. The Lady Vols shot just 23.5 percent (8 of 34) from the field and trailed by as many as 14 points. Despite the putrid performance, Summitt remained surprisingly calm during the intermission. "I didn't throw anything," she mused, "and I didn't threaten anyone."

Still down by 11 points (54–43) with 6:09 remaining, the Lady Vols suddenly exhibited the remarkable resiliency that would characterize their entire season. Outscoring the fifth-ranked Cardinal 13–2 down the stretch, Tennessee pulled even at 56–all when Davis converted a midcourt steal into a driving layup with 18 seconds left in regulation. The Lady Vols then dominated the overtime period, hitting all 6 of their field-goal tries en route to a 70–66 triumph. As usual, defense proved to be the difference for Tennessee. Stanford All-American Nicole Powell was held scoreless during the final 11:59 of regulation and missed her last 10 field-goal tries of the game.

After winning their first seven games, the Lady Vols looked entirely vulnerable again in Game 8, losing 70–60 on their home floor to Texas. The Longhorns out-rebounded Tennessee 42–27, bringing a razor edge to Summitt's postgame comments. "I can't remember the last time we were out-rebounded by fifteen," she grumbled. "I think that tells you a lot about heart and desire."

Tennessee's heart and desire improved dramatically during the next month. The Lady Vols shocked the basketball world on January 24 by stunning top-ranked Duke 72–69 in Durham. Jackson and Zolman hit 2 free throws each in the closing seconds to seal the victory and regain Summitt's approval. "Big win for our team," the coach said. "I'm really, really proud of them."

Ironically, Tennessee's greatest victory produced its greatest loss. Moore tore the anterior cruciate ligament in her left knee with just under nine minutes to go, leaving the Lady Vols with just ten scholarship players, none of whom was a true point guard. With no other viable option, Summitt switched Butts from shooting guard to the point. Knowing the move was coming didn't soften the blow for Butts, who sobbed openly. "I was hysterical," she admitted.

Summitt may have been borderline hysterical when Butts injured *her* knee against Kentucky in Tennessee's very next game. The injury proved minor, however, and Butts was back on the court in time to face Auburn on February 1. Good thing, too. Gathering up a loose ball, she sank an 8-foot jumper with 2 seconds left in regulation that knotted the score at 53–all. The Lady Vols ultimately prevailed 68–61 in overtime.

The Lady Vols didn't truly feel Moore's absence until they hosted two-time defending national champ Connecticut on February 5. The Huskies raced to a 41–30 first-half lead and were never seriously threatened on the way to a resounding 81–67 victory.

Moments after UConn ripped the Lady Vols athletically, Summitt ripped them verbally. "I would say we need to go back on the court [to practice]," she grumbled, "but NCAA rules won't allow it."

Ten days after getting their butts kicked against UConn, the Lady Vols got their Butts (Tasha) in gear against Vanderbilt. The senior guard hit 12 of 15 floor shots, including 6 of 6 from three-point range, in a career-best 37-point performance that sparked a 94–88 defeat of the homestanding Commodores.

Five days later, Zolman turned in a career-best 23-point effort to spark an 88–79 defeat of Florida. And so it went. The anticipated collapse following Moore's knee injury and the lopsided loss to UConn never materialized. Instead, those two setbacks seemed to galvanize Tennessee. The Lady Vols became an even tighter-knit team than before. This unity could be traced to seniors Robinson, Butts, Davis, and McDaniel. Since none had won first-team All-America recognition and none had won a national title, they were widely viewed as an undistinguished signing class. These seniors wore the orange proudly, however, and they were determined to wear it all the way to the Final Four.

"We basically wrapped our arms around the program," Butts said. "We've been here for the program. I hope people realize that we have been here to help Tennessee."

Fans who had forgotten that soon would be reminded in dramatic fashion. When McDaniel left the team due to nagging medical problems the week of the regular-season finale, Tennessee's roster was reduced to nine scholarship players. Following an overtime loss to Georgia in the Southeastern Conference tournament, however, the Lady Vols' three remaining seniors picked the team up and carried it to the Final Four.

Robinson recorded her first double-double of the season (13 points, 11 rebounds, plus 5 blocked shots) as Tennessee hammered Colgate 77–54 in Round 1 of the NCAA Tournament.

Davis recorded the first double-double of her career (12 points, 10 rebounds) as the Lady Vols belted DePaul 79–59 in Round 2, sending them into the Sweet 16.

Butts hit a pair of game-winning free throws with two-tenths of a second remaining, providing a 71–69 defeat of Baylor in Round 3. Six minutes earlier, the Lady Vols had appeared doomed when Robinson fouled out with Baylor on top 65–57. As tears trickled down her cheeks, Robinson begged her teammates: "Don't let this be my last game."

They didn't. Tennessee outscored the Bears 12–2 to take a 69–67 lead with 1:37 left. Baylor tied the score moments later, and it was still 69–all with 10 seconds to go. That's when Davis intercepted a pass and lobbed to Ely, who blew a driving layup. Following the play, Davis blew the putback, but an official blew his whistle when Baylor's Jessika Stratton bumped Butts as they scrambled for the loose ball. After viewing the video replay several times, officials determined Butts had been fouled a split second before the final horn sounded. Undaunted by the delays and a chorus of boos, she coolly drained her free throws to seal the deal.

"I had ice water in my veins," she said.

Zolman called the finish "very surreal." She couldn't have known it at the time, but the surreal stuff was just beginning.

Stanford raced to a 26–18 lead in the Elite Eight round, but the never-say-die Lady Vols came roaring back. The nerve-wracking game featured nine lead changes and nine ties—the last at 60–60. At this point Butts saved the day for the second game in a row, hitting a leaning shot with 1.7 seconds left to cap a thrilling 62–60 victory. The seniors had their wish: Tennessee was in the Final Four.

Following their usual postseason script in their semifinal game, the Lady Vols played like chumps at the start—trailing Louisiana State 25–19 at the half—then played like champs at its finish. Tied at 50 with 6 seconds left and LSU in possession of the ball, Tennessee made a clutch steal and Davis made a slow-motion layup with 1.2 seconds left for a 52–50 win. "I knew it was a slow release," Davis explained, "but I just wanted to make sure it went in."

It went in all right, and the Lady Vols went on — to the national championship game. There they would face superstar Diana Taurasi and two-time defending national champ UConn. Racing to a 30–13 lead, the tall and talented Huskies appeared ready to put Tennessee away early. The scrappy Lady Vols scored the final 11 points of the first half, however, closing to 30–24 by intermission.

Ely had been playing throughout March on an injured foot and two sore knees. Once UConn coach Geno Auriemma realized this, he rerouted his offense toward the basket to exploit Ely's limitations. The ploy worked, and the Huskies went on to prevail 70–61. Although the Huskies won the title, it was the Lady Vols who won much of the praise. "This team is full of tough kids," Auriemma said. "I have so much respect for Pat's program and what they did this season."

Even the hard-to-please Summitt saluted her disappointed troops. "We've had a great season and a great run," she said. "I hope that when they reflect on this year, they realize how they grew as a team. They are one of the most determined, most ambitious teams I have coached in a long time."

Although the starless, point guard–less Lady Vols fell one step short of the national title, they proved one point conclusively: You don't have to win a championship to be a champion.